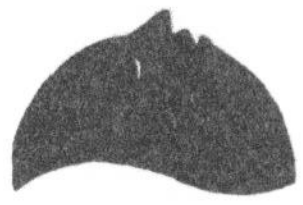

Dedicated to Frank and May Baskeyfield

Blurb written by Rose Cartwright.

Special thanks to Ma, Pa,
Richard and Elizabeth Hunter
and to Sam and Alex for letting me
tell another story.

MAP
OF
DAYS

Prologue

Map of Days

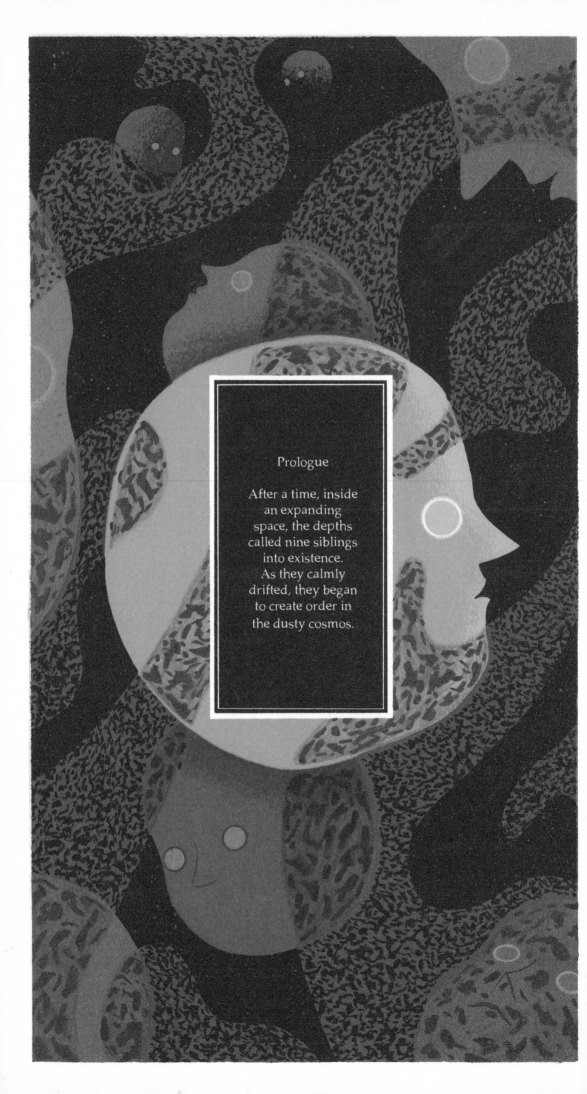

Prologue

After a time, inside
an expanding
space, the depths
called nine siblings
into existence.
As they calmly
drifted, they began
to create order in
the dusty cosmos.

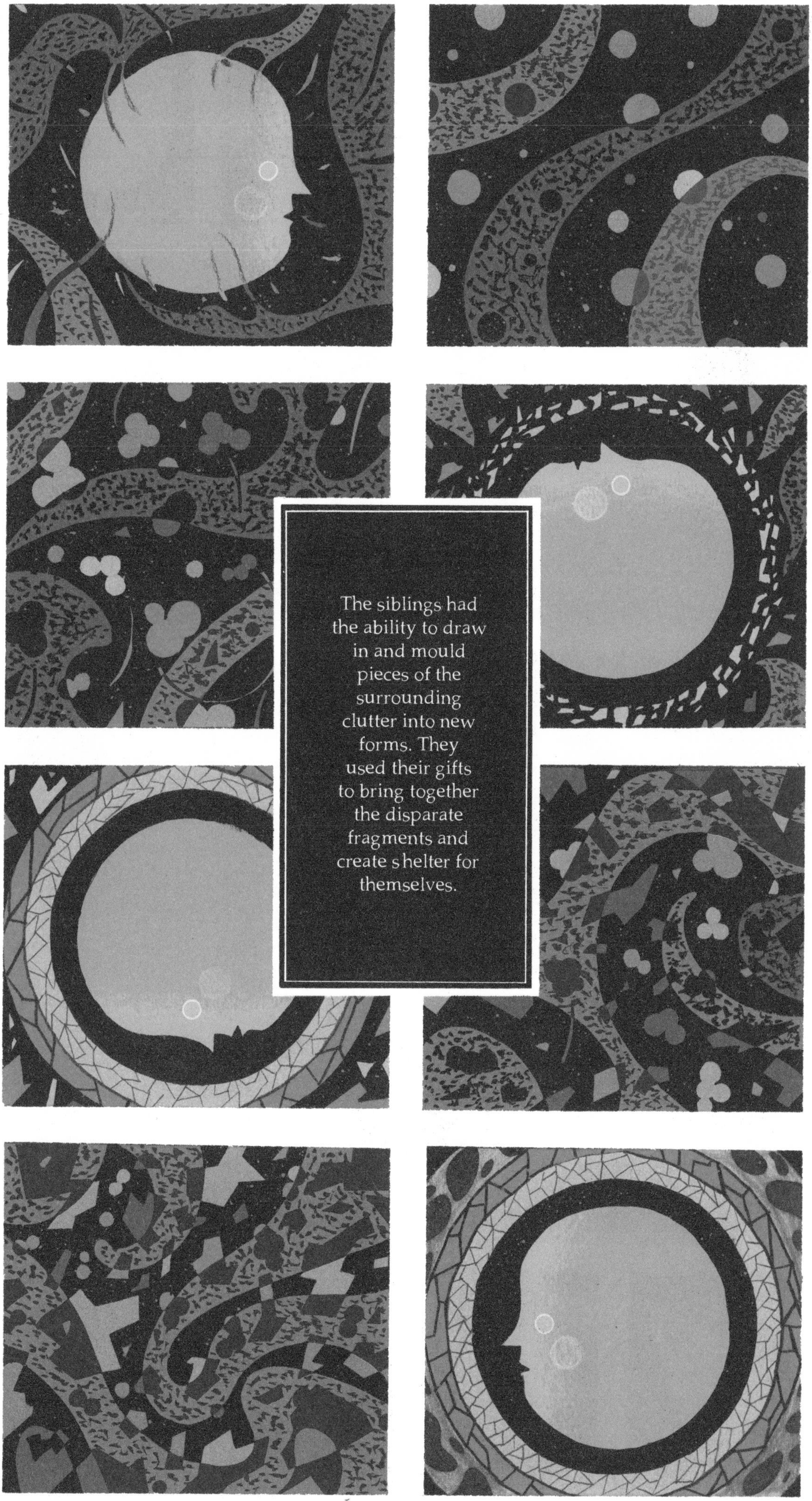
The siblings had the ability to draw in and mould pieces of the surrounding clutter into new forms. They used their gifts to bring together the disparate fragments and create shelter for themselves.

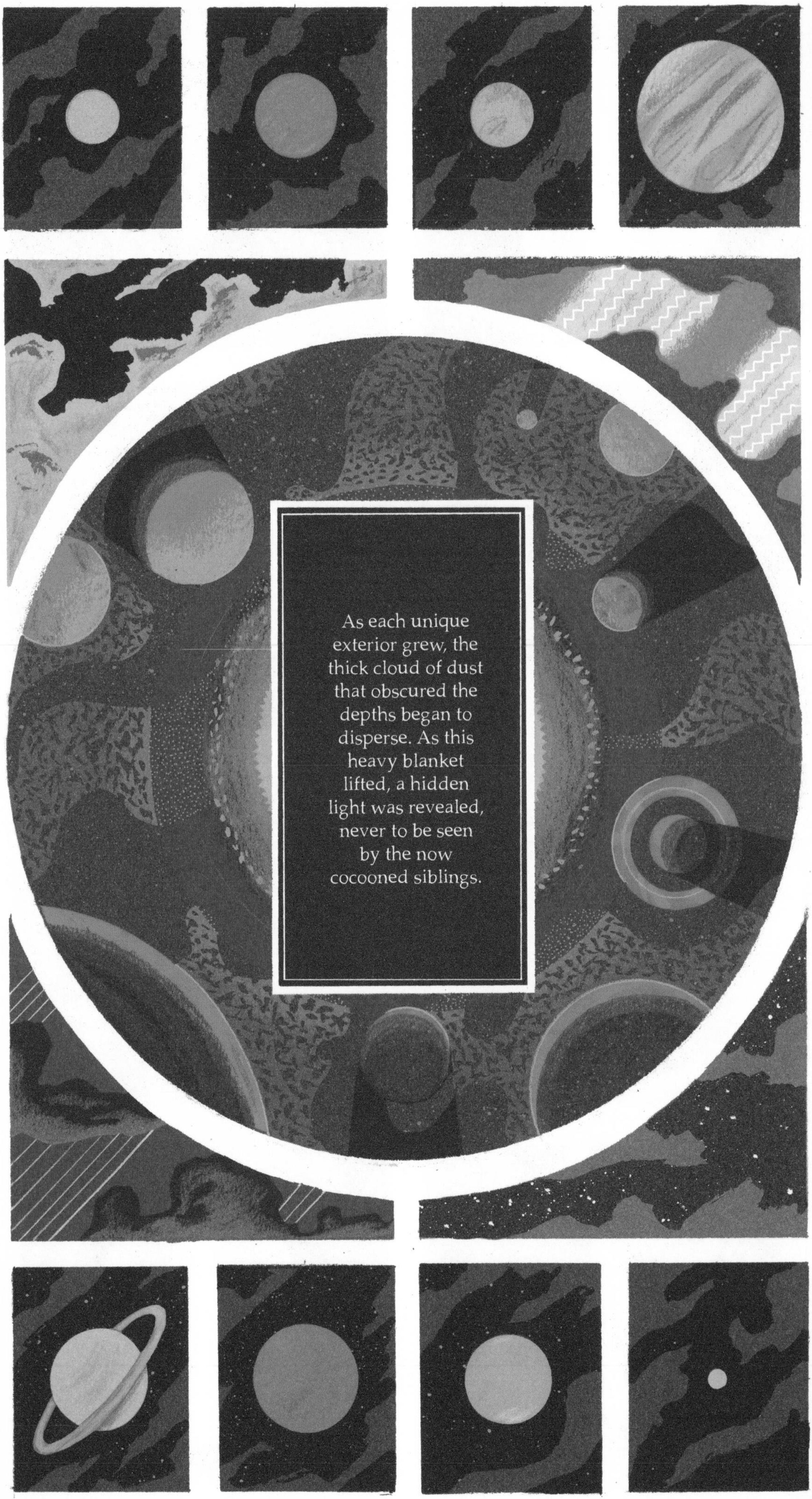

As each unique exterior grew, the thick cloud of dust that obscured the depths began to disperse. As this heavy blanket lifted, a hidden light was revealed, never to be seen by the now cocooned siblings.

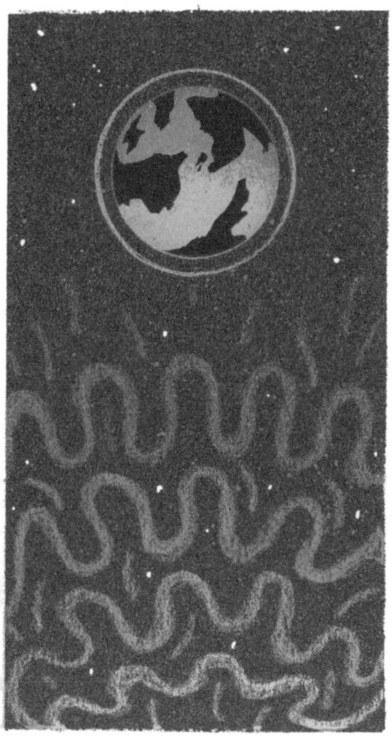

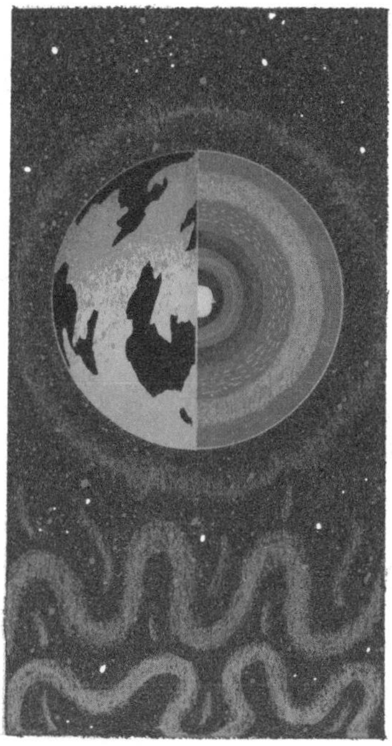

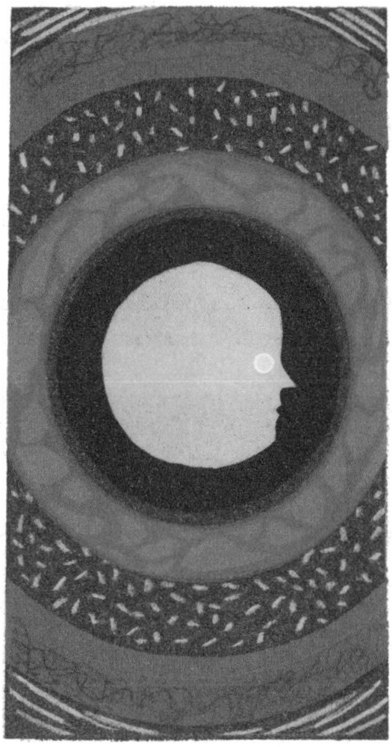

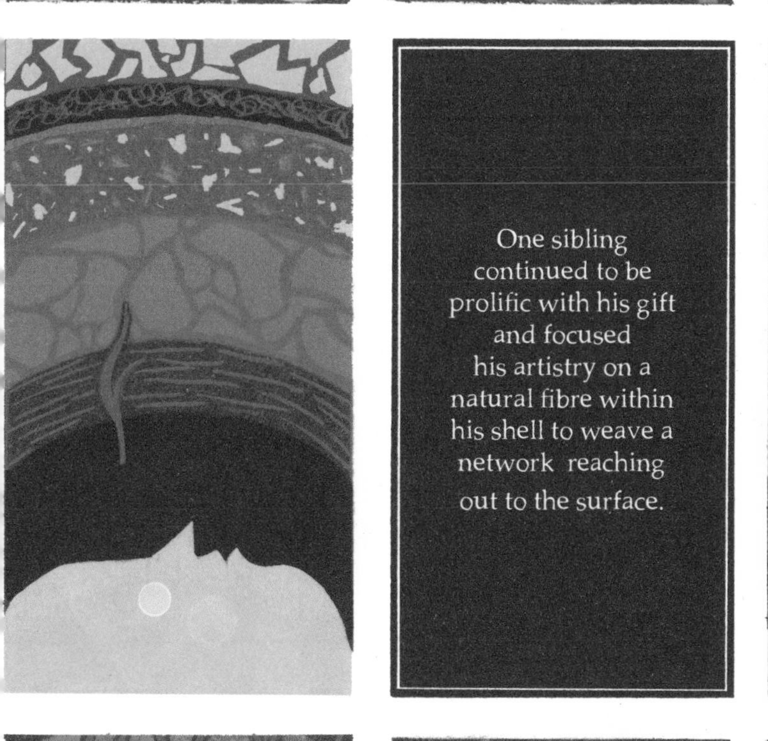

One sibling continued to be prolific with his gift and focused his artistry on a natural fibre within his shell to weave a network reaching out to the surface.

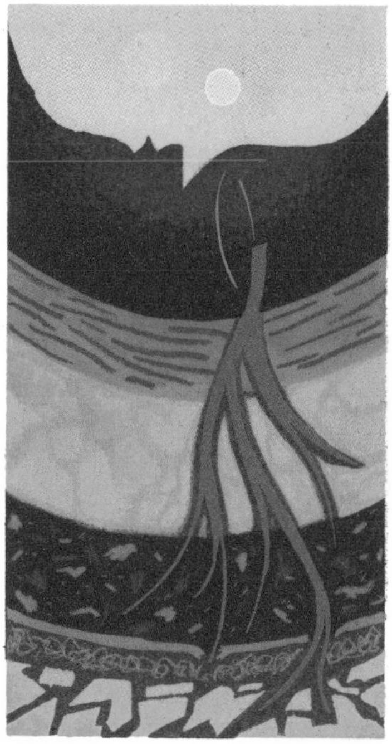

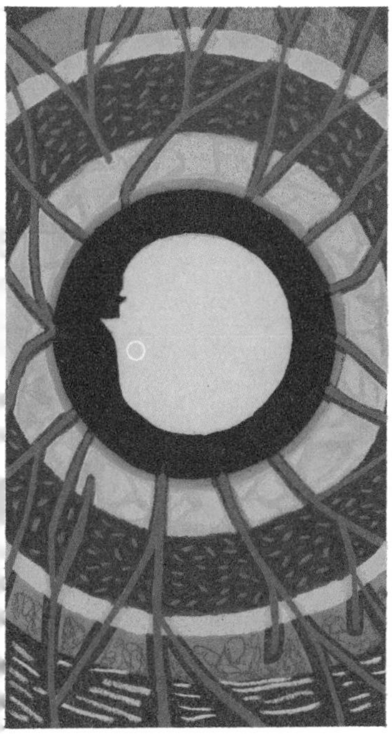

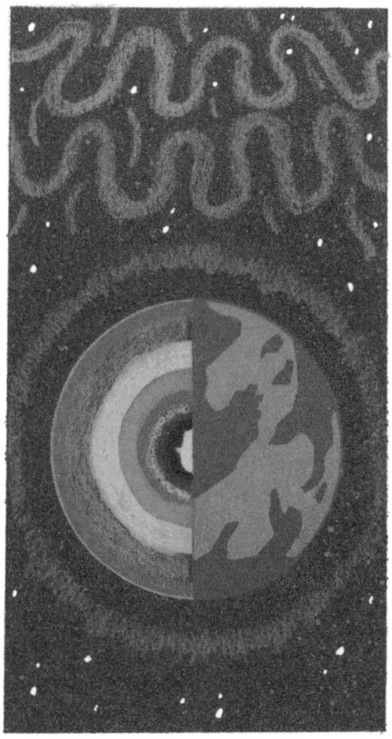

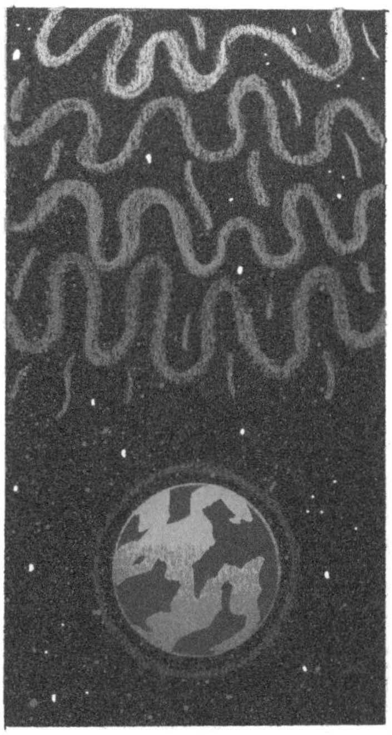

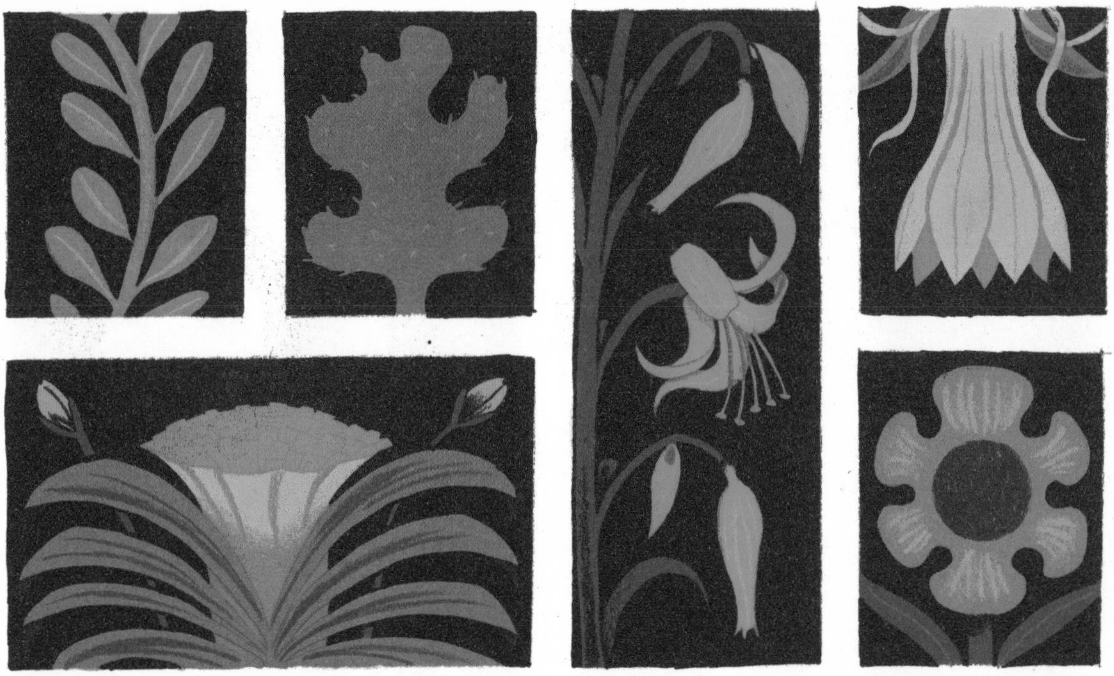

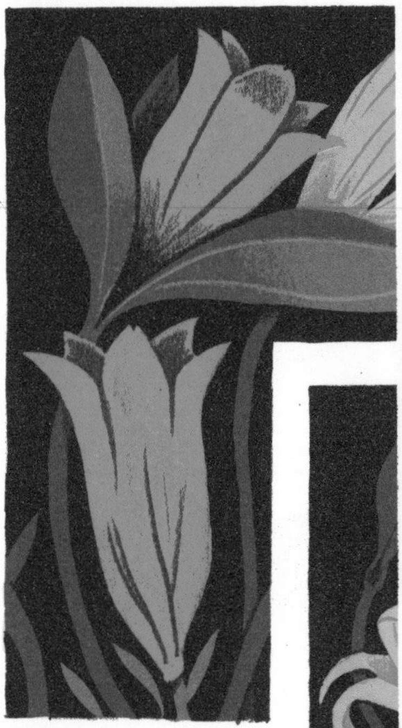

Once these extensions broke free from the layered cocoon, they transformed into countless beautiful and complex shapes. As they grew ever larger and reached out ever further, these extensions of his being began to send signals back to their creator.

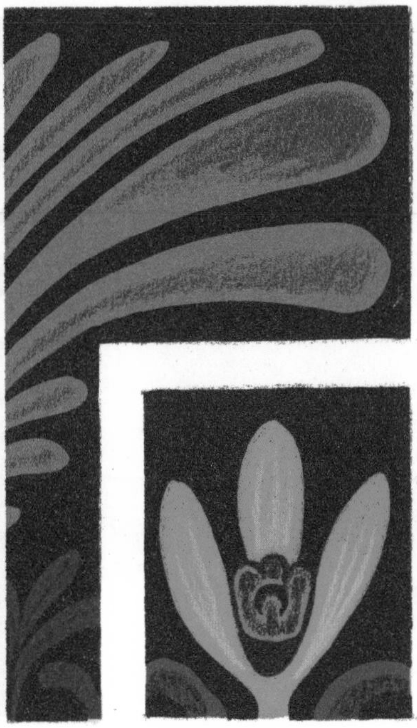

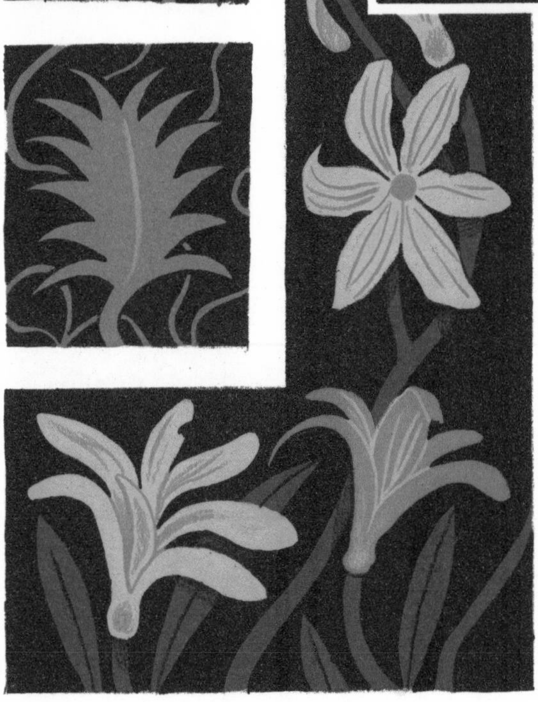

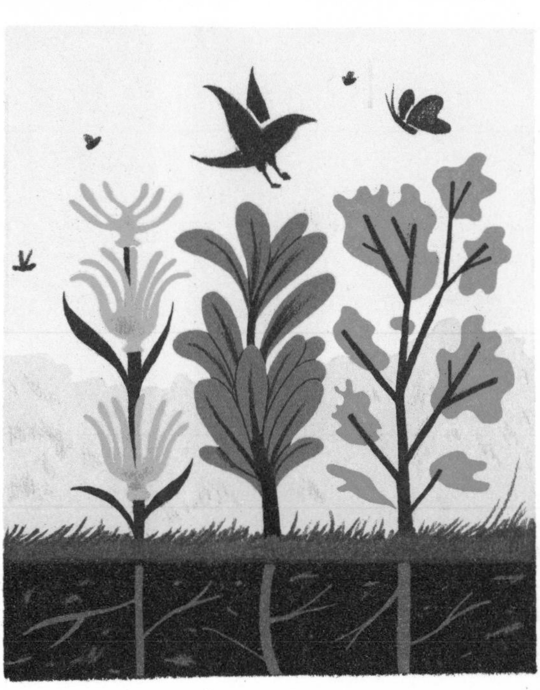

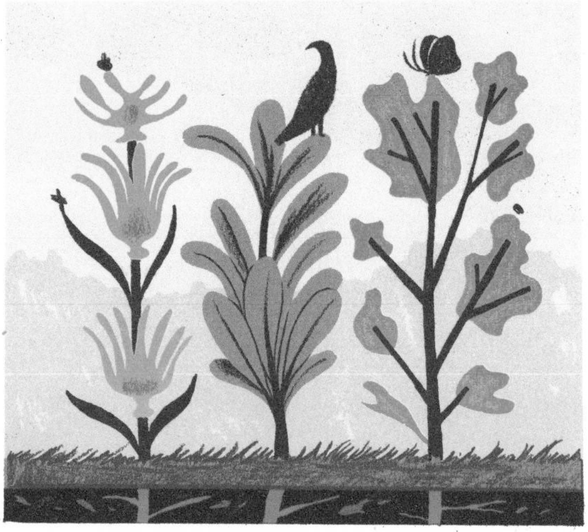

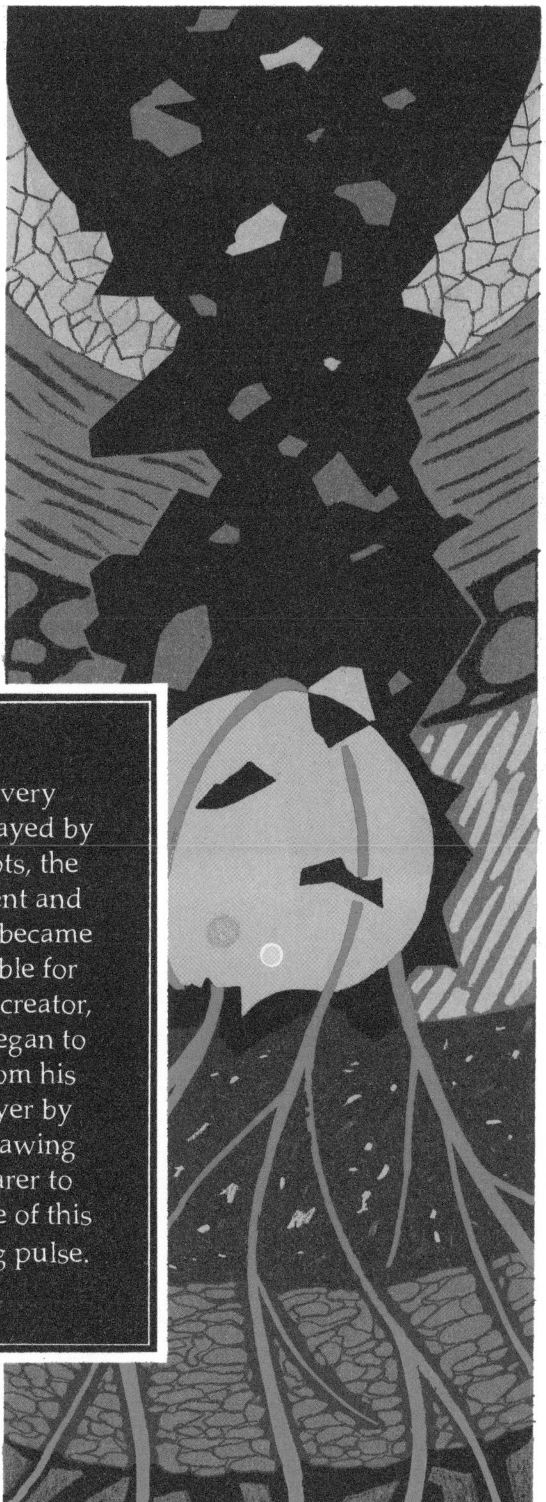

With every signal relayed by their roots, the excitement and curiosity became unbearable for the blind creator, and he began to erupt from his shell, layer by layer, drawing ever nearer to the source of this intriguing pulse.

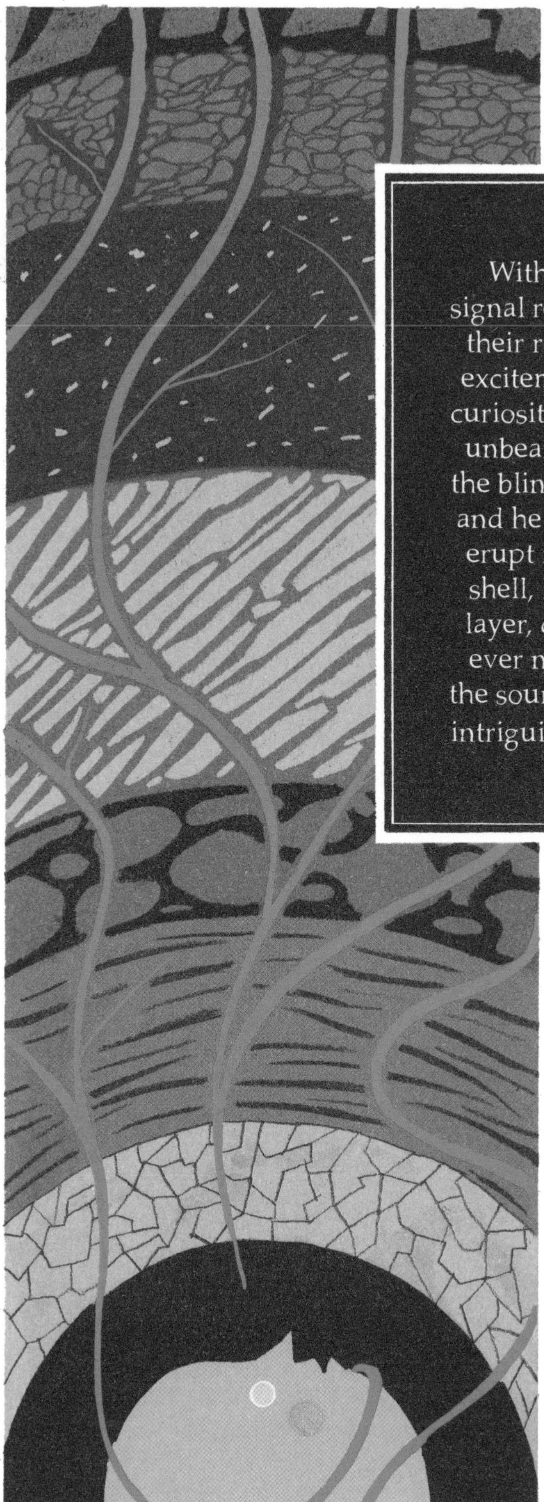

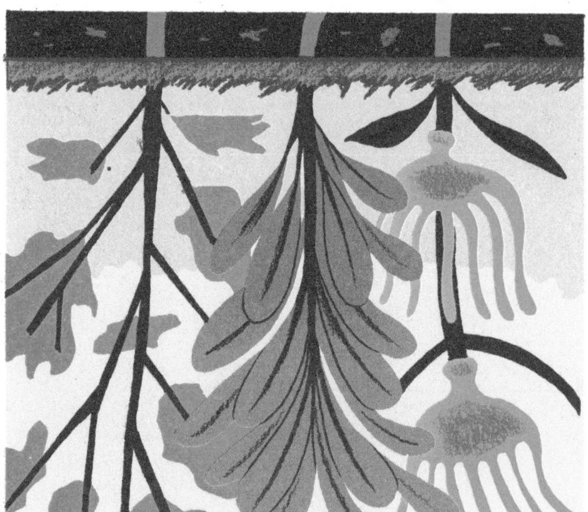

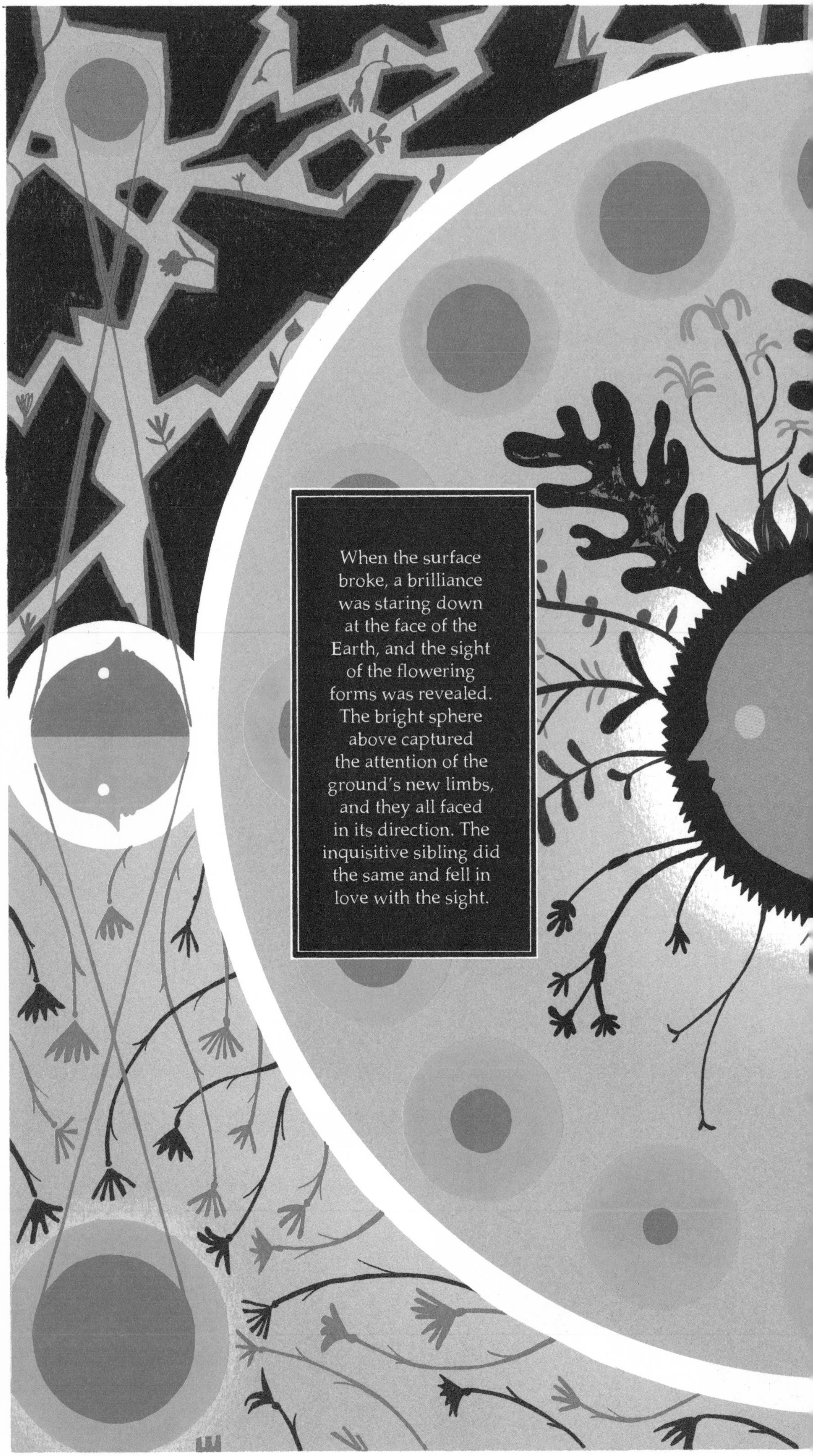

When the surface broke, a brilliance was staring down at the face of the Earth, and the sight of the flowering forms was revealed. The bright sphere above captured the attention of the ground's new limbs, and they all faced in its direction. The inquisitive sibling did the same and fell in love with the sight.

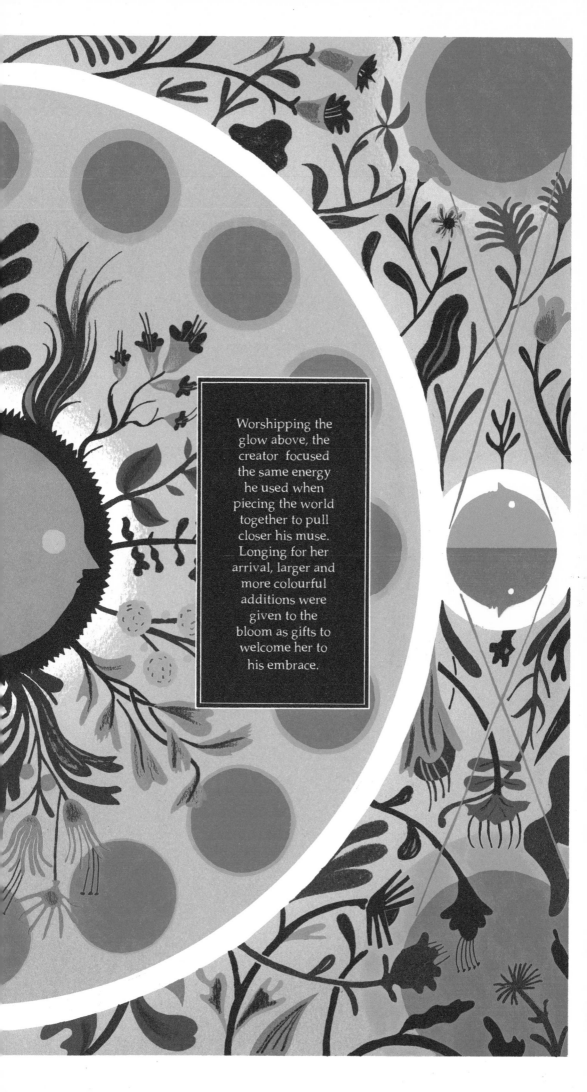

Worshipping the
glow above, the
creator focused
the same energy
he used when
piecing the world
together to pull
closer his muse.
Longing for her
arrival, larger and
more colourful
additions were
given to the
bloom as gifts to
welcome her to
his embrace.

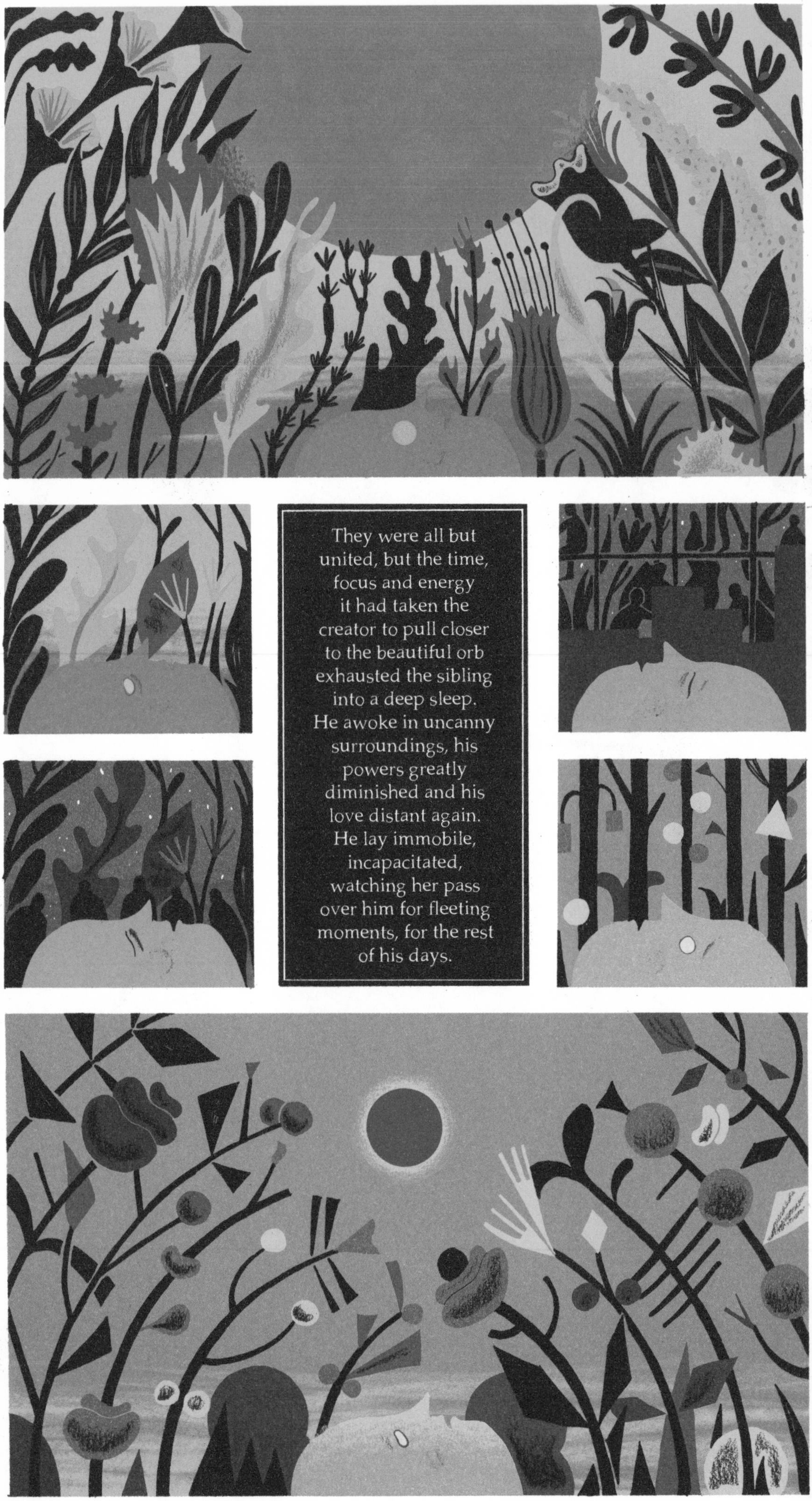
They were all but united, but the time, focus and energy it had taken the creator to pull closer to the beautiful orb exhausted the sibling into a deep sleep. He awoke in uncanny surroundings, his powers greatly diminished and his love distant again. He lay immobile, incapacitated, watching her pass over him for fleeting moments, for the rest of his days.

Map of Days

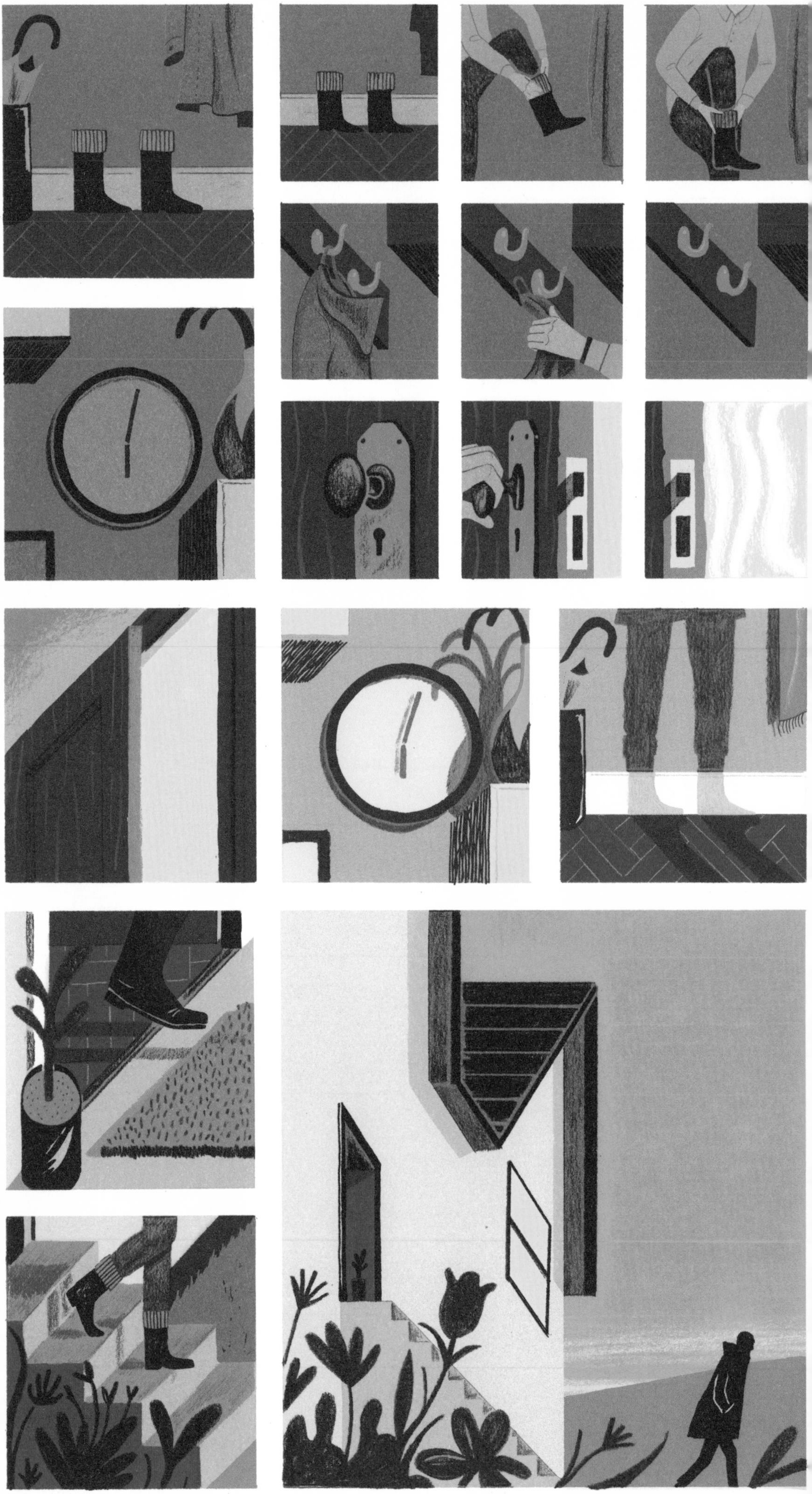

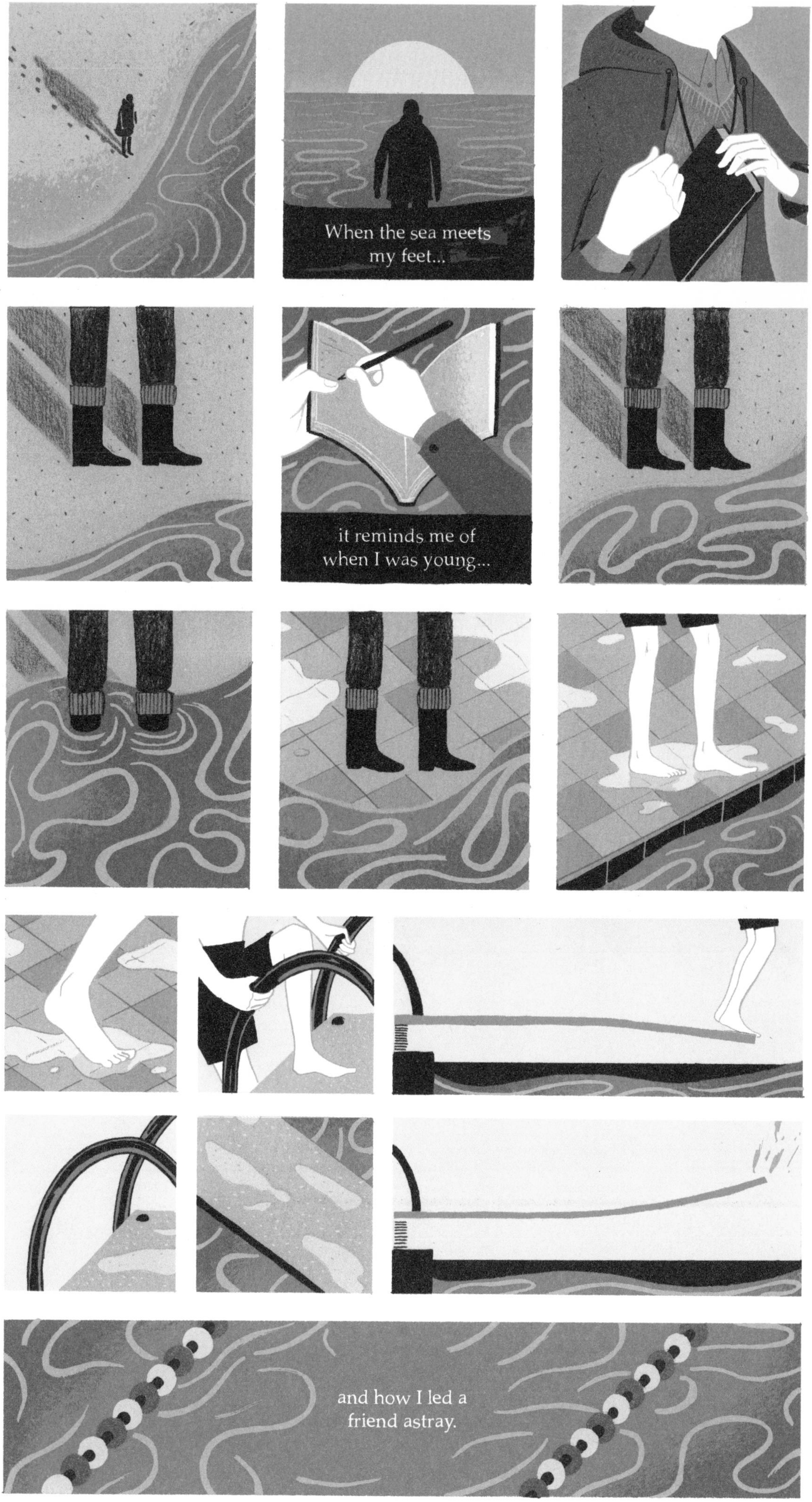
When the sea meets my feet...
it reminds me of when I was young...
and how I led a friend astray.

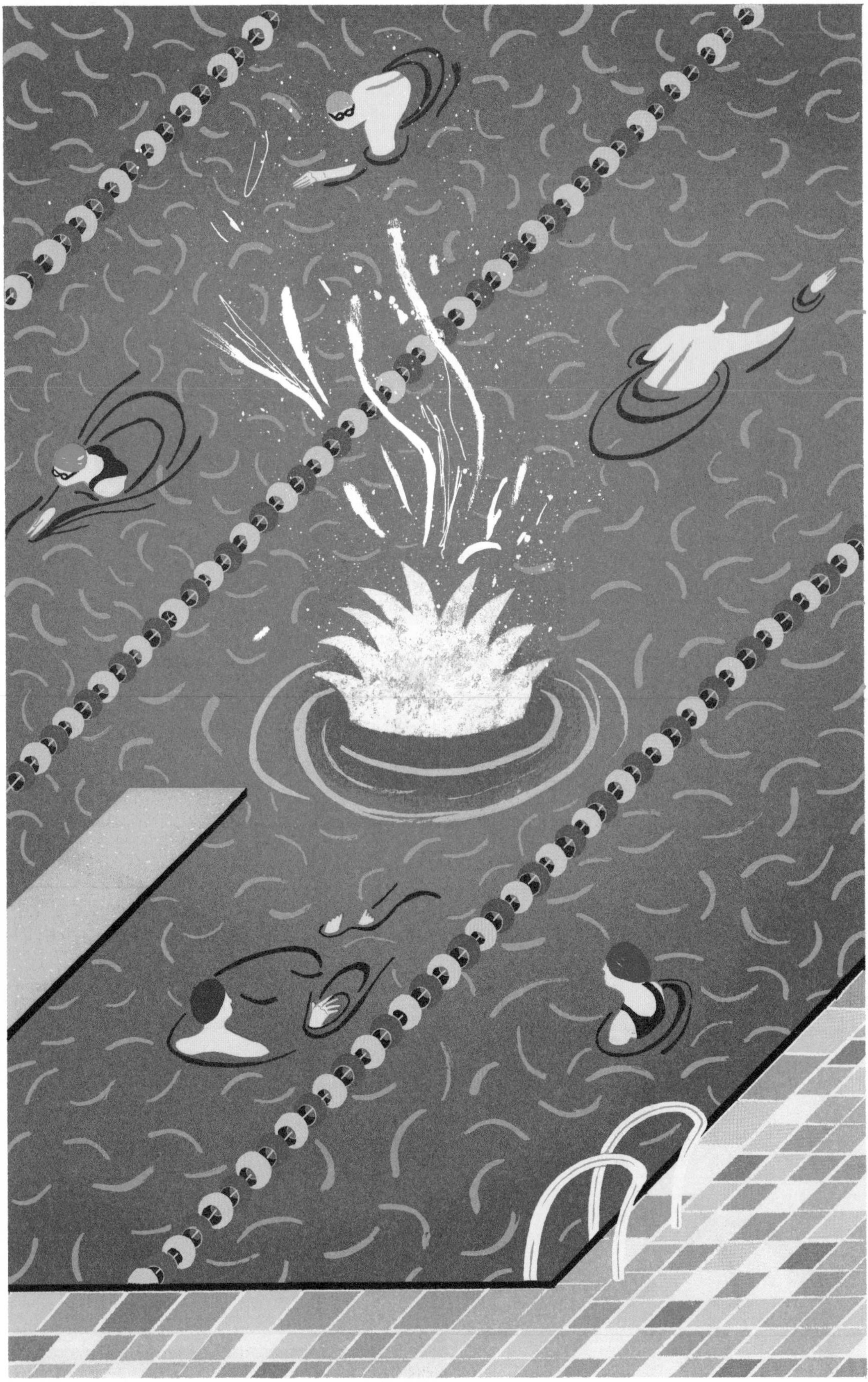

I used to attend swimming lessons. One week the lesson involved retrieving a rubber brick from the bottom of the pool and swimming in our pyjamas. I couldn't understand when I'd ever need to swim wearing pyjamas, and using them in the lesson meant that I wouldn't be able to wear them that night at my grandfather Frank's.

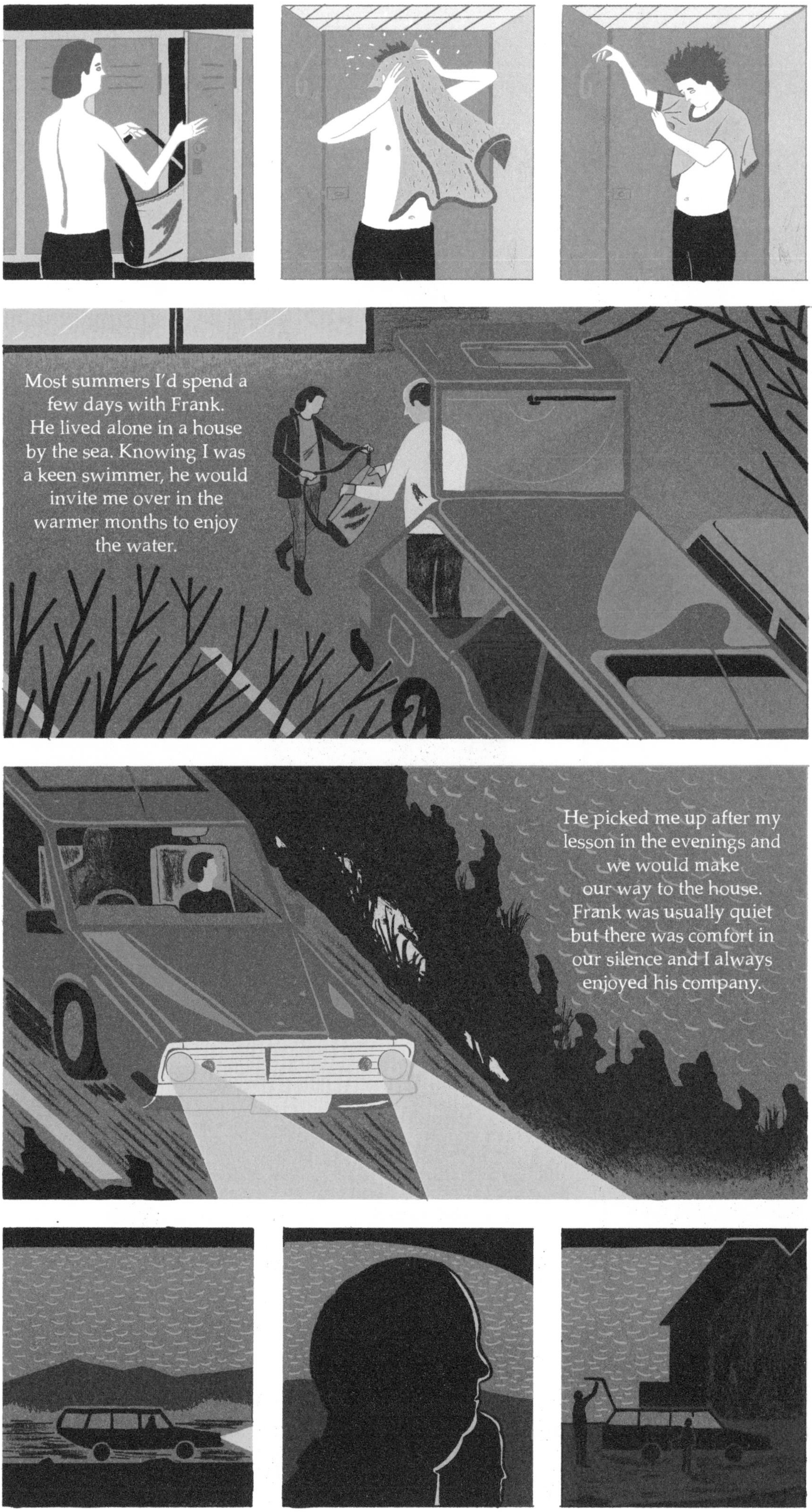
Most summers I'd spend a few days with Frank. He lived alone in a house by the sea. Knowing I was a keen swimmer, he would invite me over in the warmer months to enjoy the water.
He picked me up after my lesson in the evenings and we would make our way to the house. Frank was usually quiet but there was comfort in our silence and I always enjoyed his company.

The interior of the house was decorated with a vast collection of objects.
One collection dominated the space, the grandfather clocks.

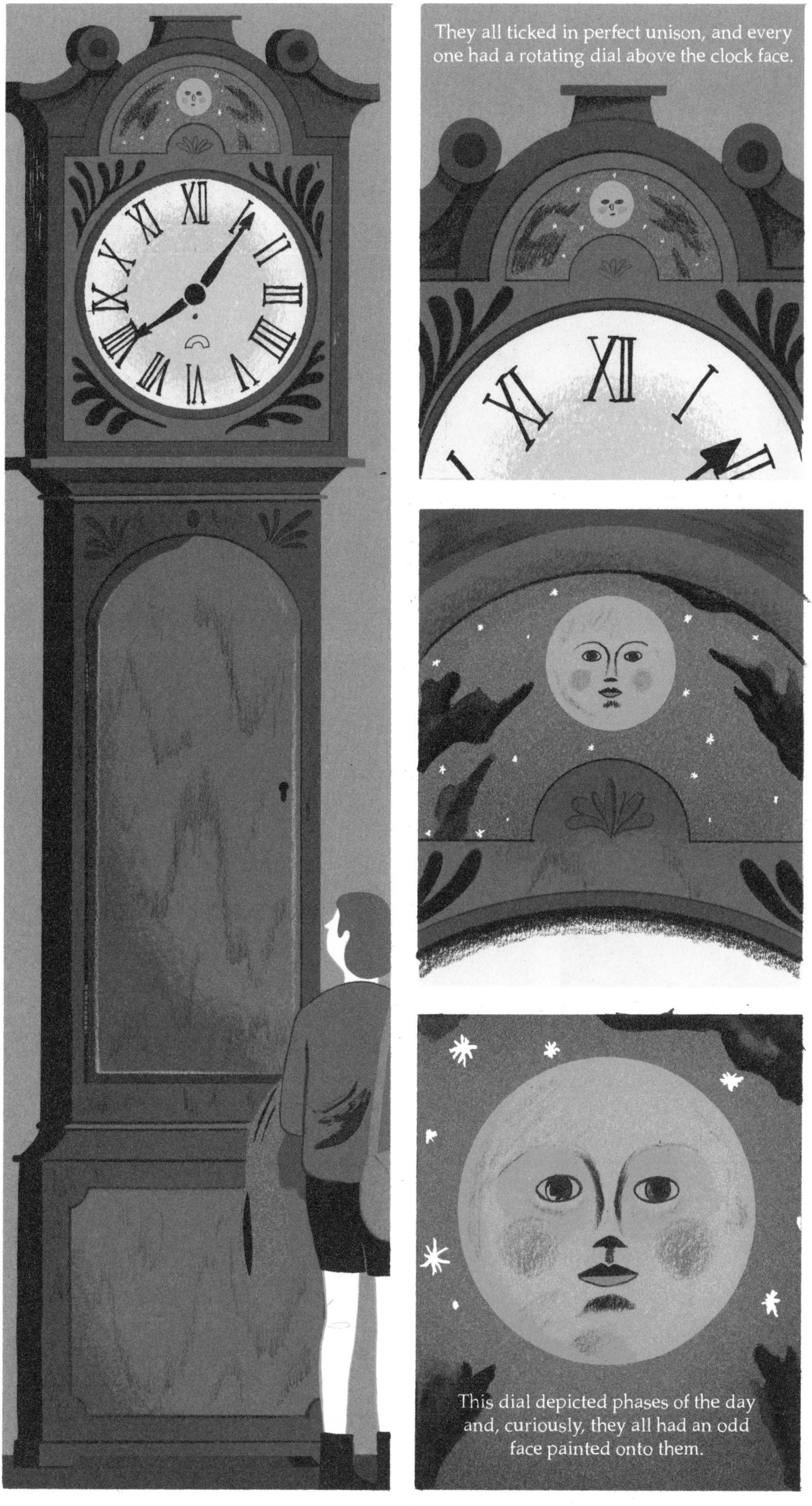
They all ticked in perfect unison, and every one had a rotating dial above the clock face.
This dial depicted phases of the day and, curiously, they all had an odd face painted onto them.

Adjusting to the chorus of ticking throughout the night was difficult, and Frank's morning routine made it impossible to sleep in.

The terrible winding noise would echo around the house.

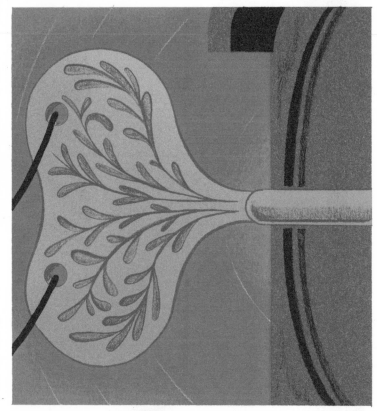

Frank would obsessively calibrate the grandfather clocks to sync with one another, using a key he always kept around his neck. I couldn't understand why.

On this particular
stay I had agreed to
help with gardening.
Frank's garden,
much like his house,
was a collection of
strange, varied and
beautiful forms.

After a few hours we
were interrupted.

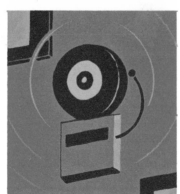

An alarm sounded from
within the house.

The ringing distracted
Frank and I
from our work.
In a panicked flurry,
Frank dashed back
towards the house and
insisted I stay outside
until his return.

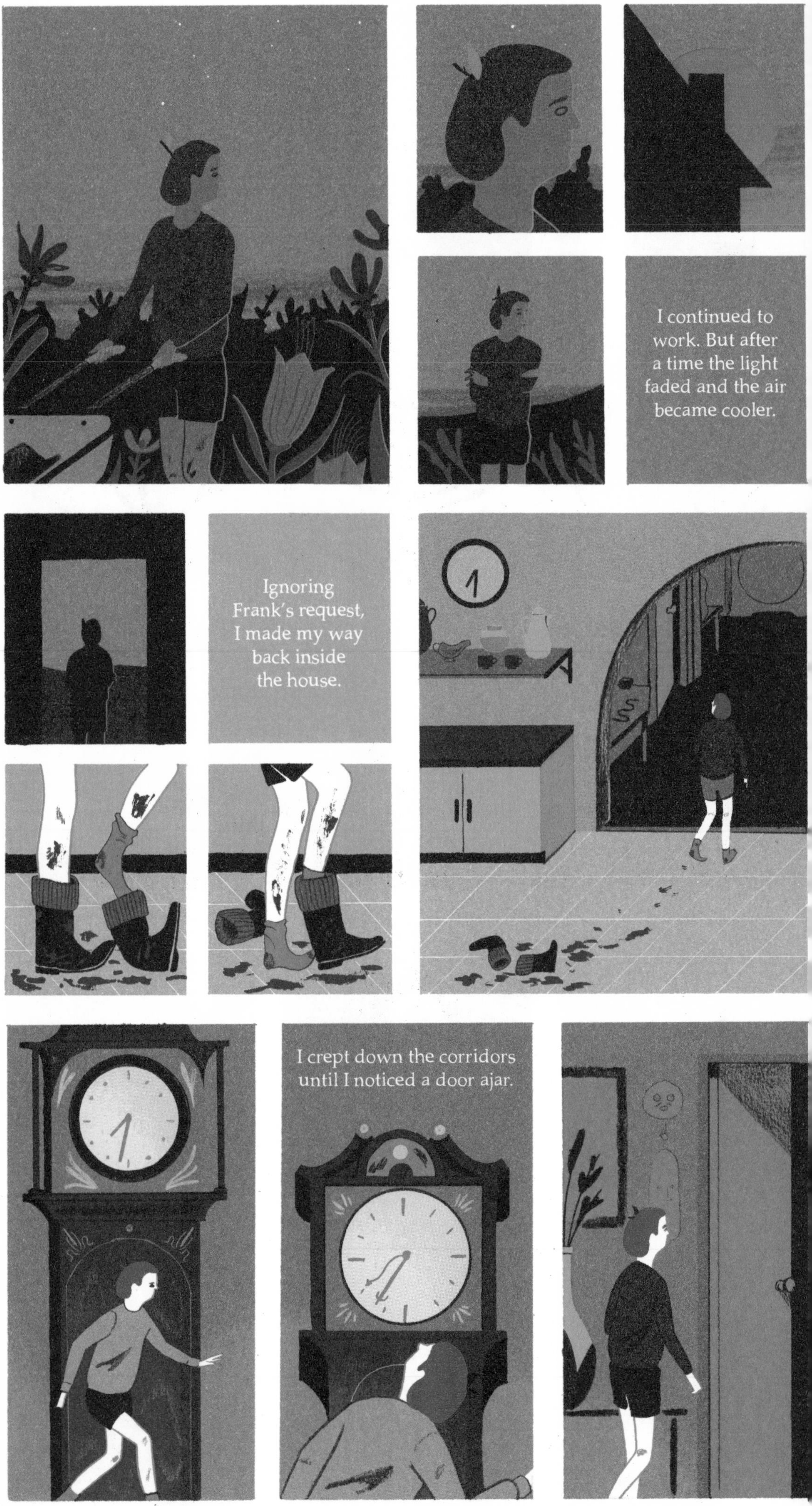
I continued to work. But after a time the light faded and the air became cooler.
Ignoring Frank's request, I made my way back inside the house.
I crept down the corridors until I noticed a door ajar.

The door was to Frank's workshop, a room that until that day had been a mystery to me.

Amongst the tools and equipment I found detailed plans for some kind of construction.

I was worried about being caught, but couldn't stop looking at the intricate drawings.

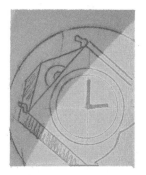

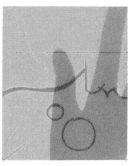

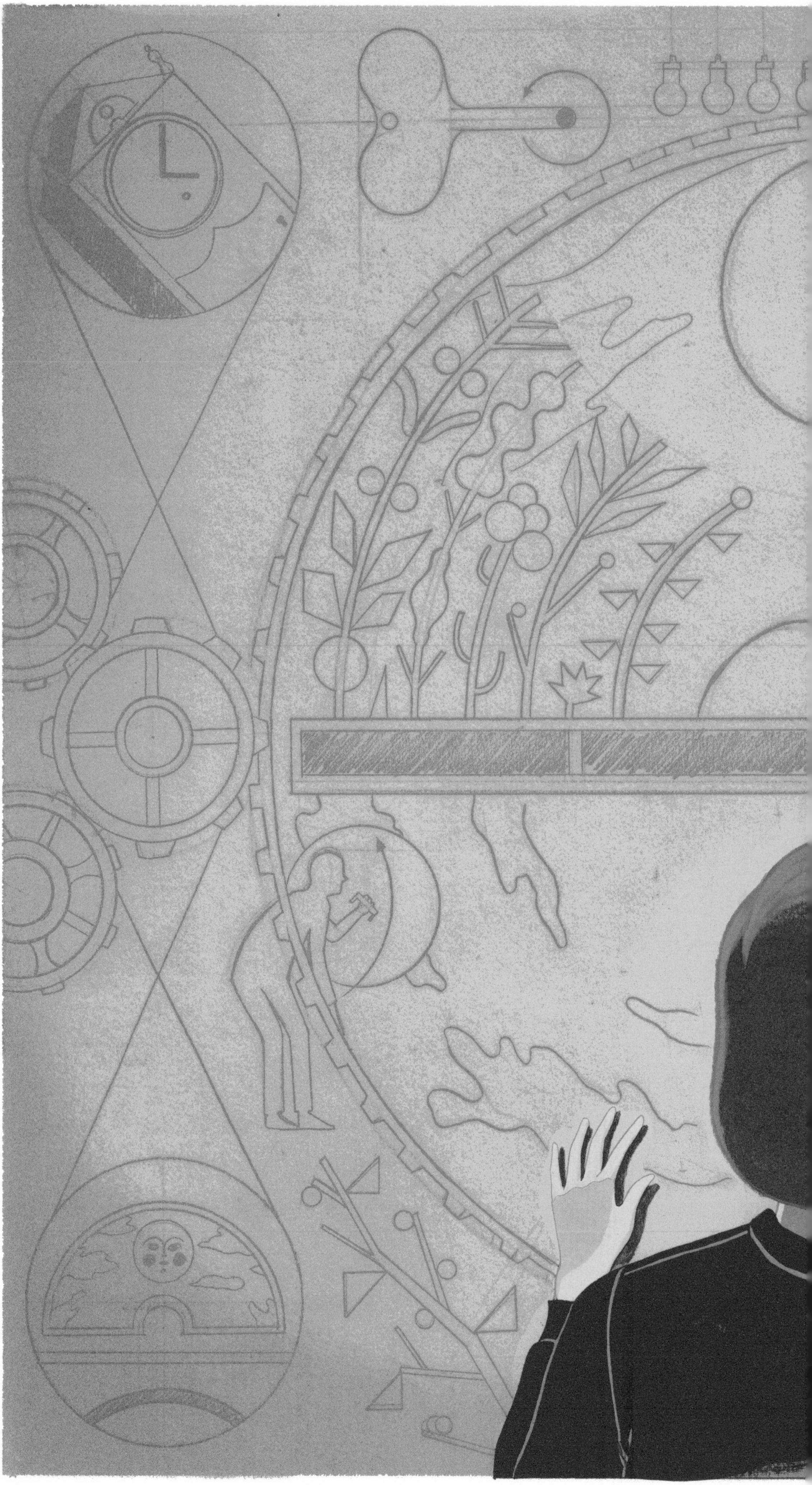

MAP OF DAYS

I heard a muffled clanging noise come from the hallway. I became nervous and wanted to leave the workshop.

I desperately tried to reset anything I had moved and inched towards the door. I was struck by an odd sight.

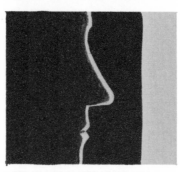

Frank seemed distracted and flustered as he emerged from the grandfather clock.

In his haste, the key was left in the clock's door and Frank flitted down the corridor, away from his workshop, and from me.

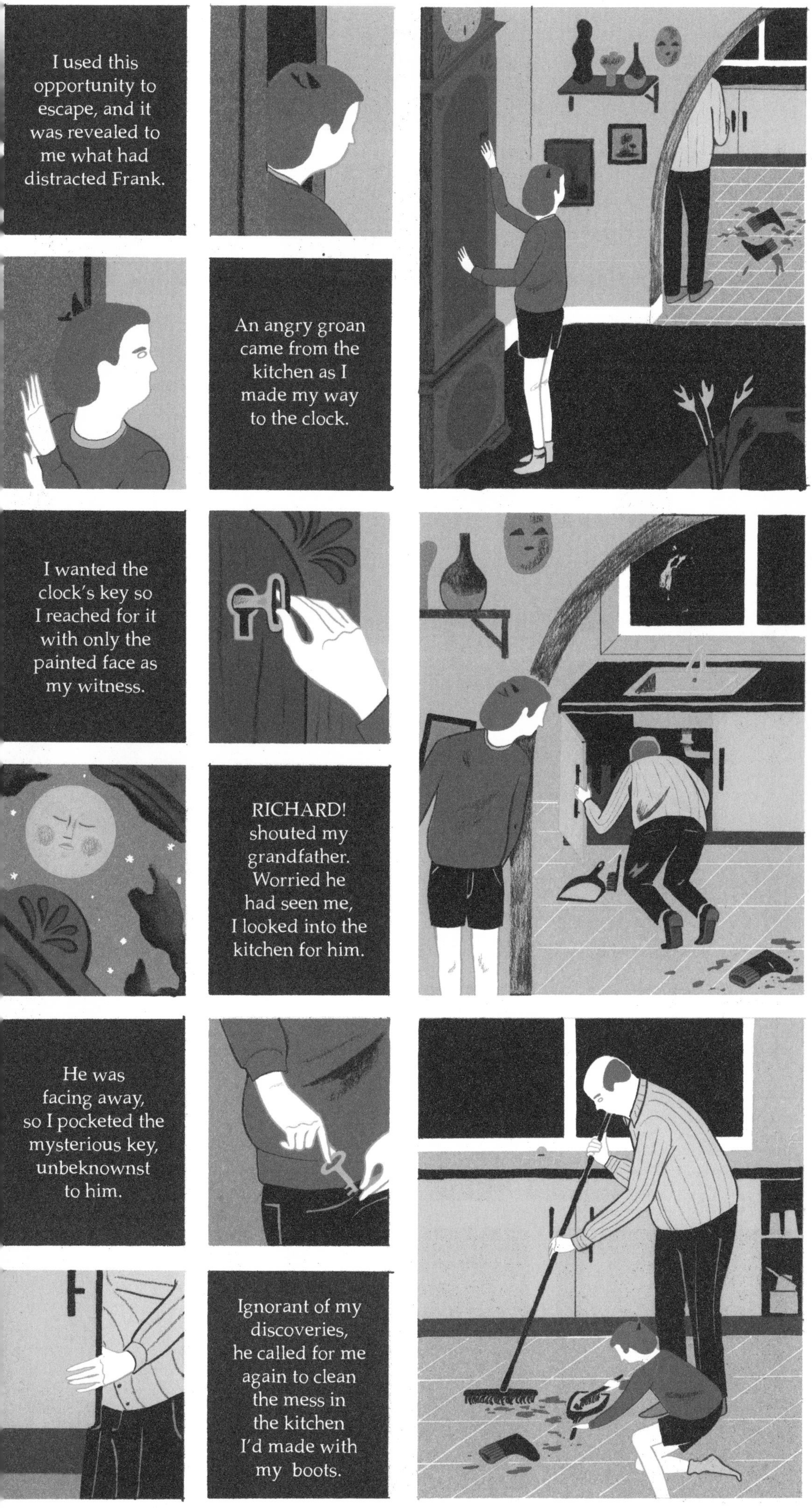
I used this opportunity to escape, and it was revealed to me what had distracted Frank.
An angry groan came from the kitchen as I made my way to the clock.
I wanted the clock's key so I reached for it with only the painted face as my witness.
RICHARD! shouted my grandfather. Worried he had seen me, I looked into the kitchen for him.
He was facing away, so I pocketed the mysterious key, unbeknownst to him.
Ignorant of my discoveries, he called for me again to clean the mess in the kitchen I'd made with my boots.

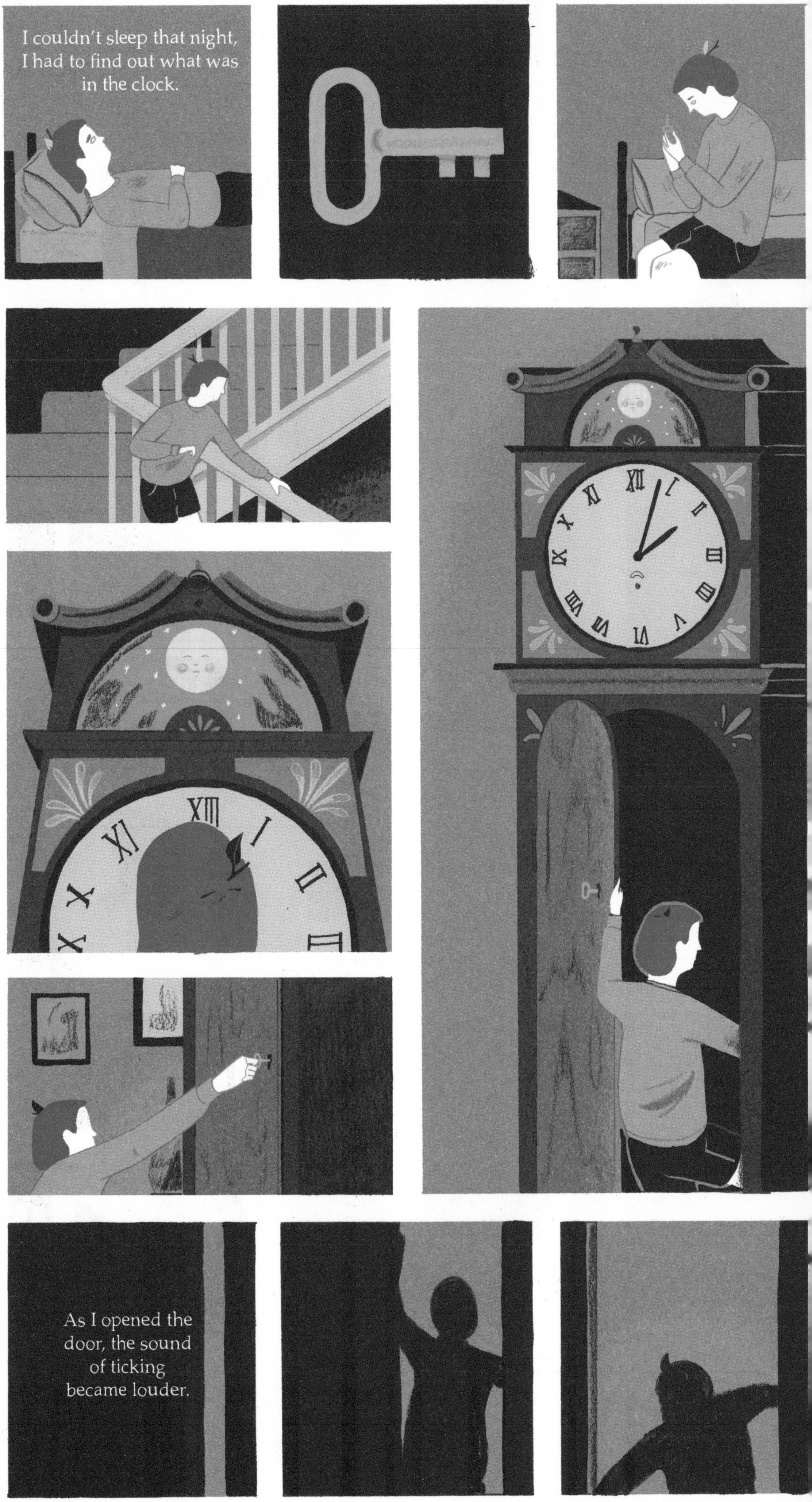
I couldn't sleep that night, I had to find out what was in the clock.
As I opened the door, the sound of ticking became louder.

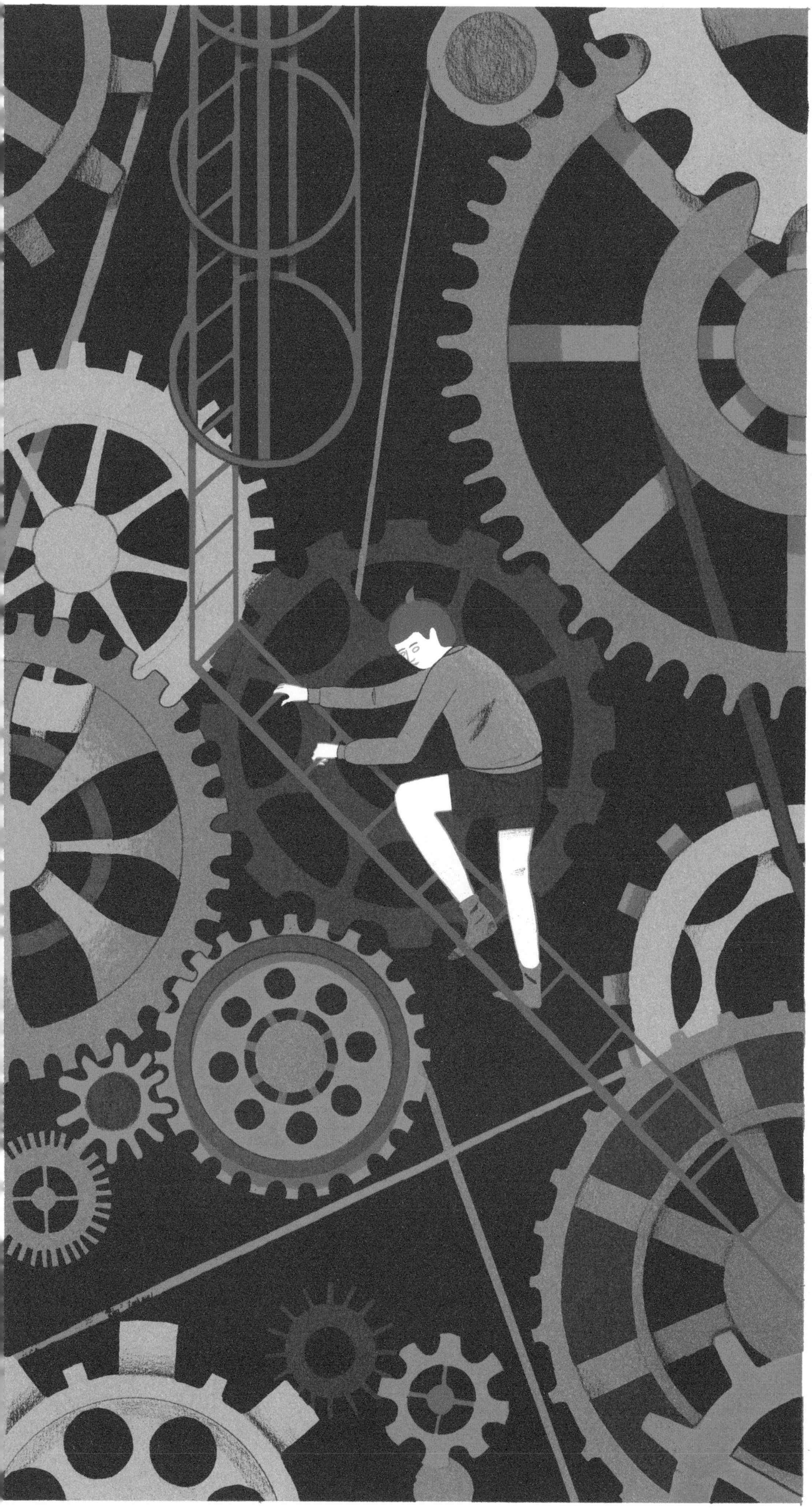

With every cog turn,
a large surface shifted.

I couldn't help wondering if
this was why all the clocks
had to be synchronised?

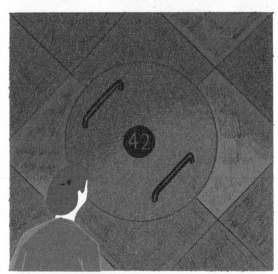

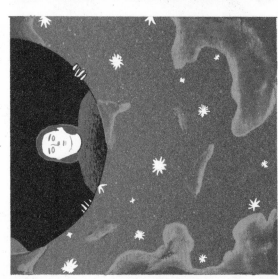

Through one of many
openings, I peered down
into a dark room.
As my pupils adjusted,
tall formations came
into view.

There were handles, almost like a ladder, leading to the floor. As my sight adjusted further, I could see what looked like an evening sky all around me, with a thick brush covering the ground.

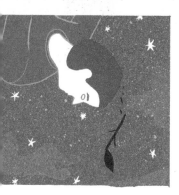

As I looked down through the brush, something fell from me.

It landed just next to what seemed like a sleeping face. It stirred and I clambered back up the ladder and out of the strange room as quickly as I could.

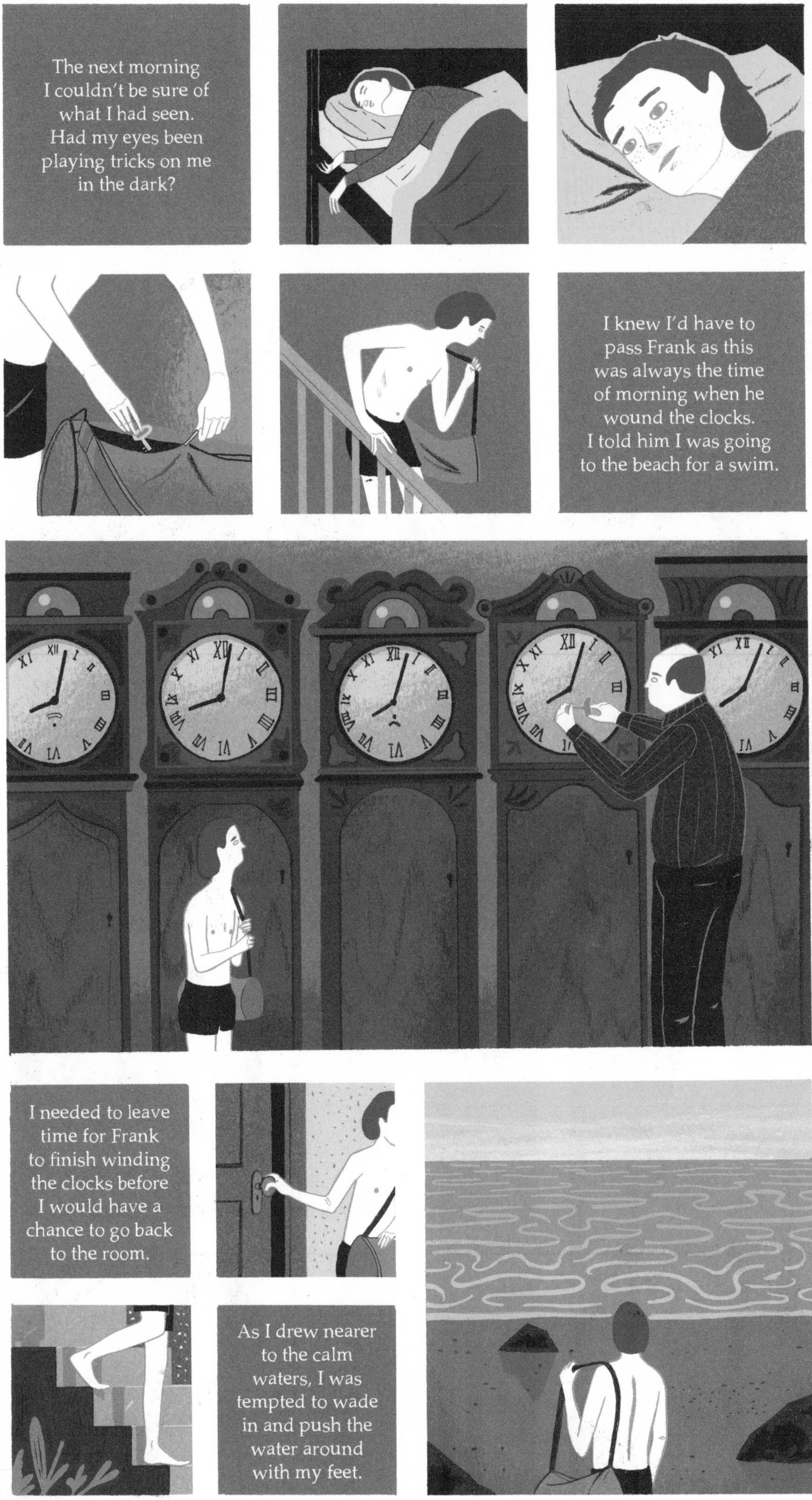
The next morning I couldn't be sure of what I had seen. Had my eyes been playing tricks on me in the dark?
I knew I'd have to pass Frank as this was always the time of morning when he wound the clocks. I told him I was going to the beach for a swim.
I needed to leave time for Frank to finish winding the clocks before I would have a chance to go back to the room.
As I drew nearer to the calm waters, I was tempted to wade in and push the water around with my feet.

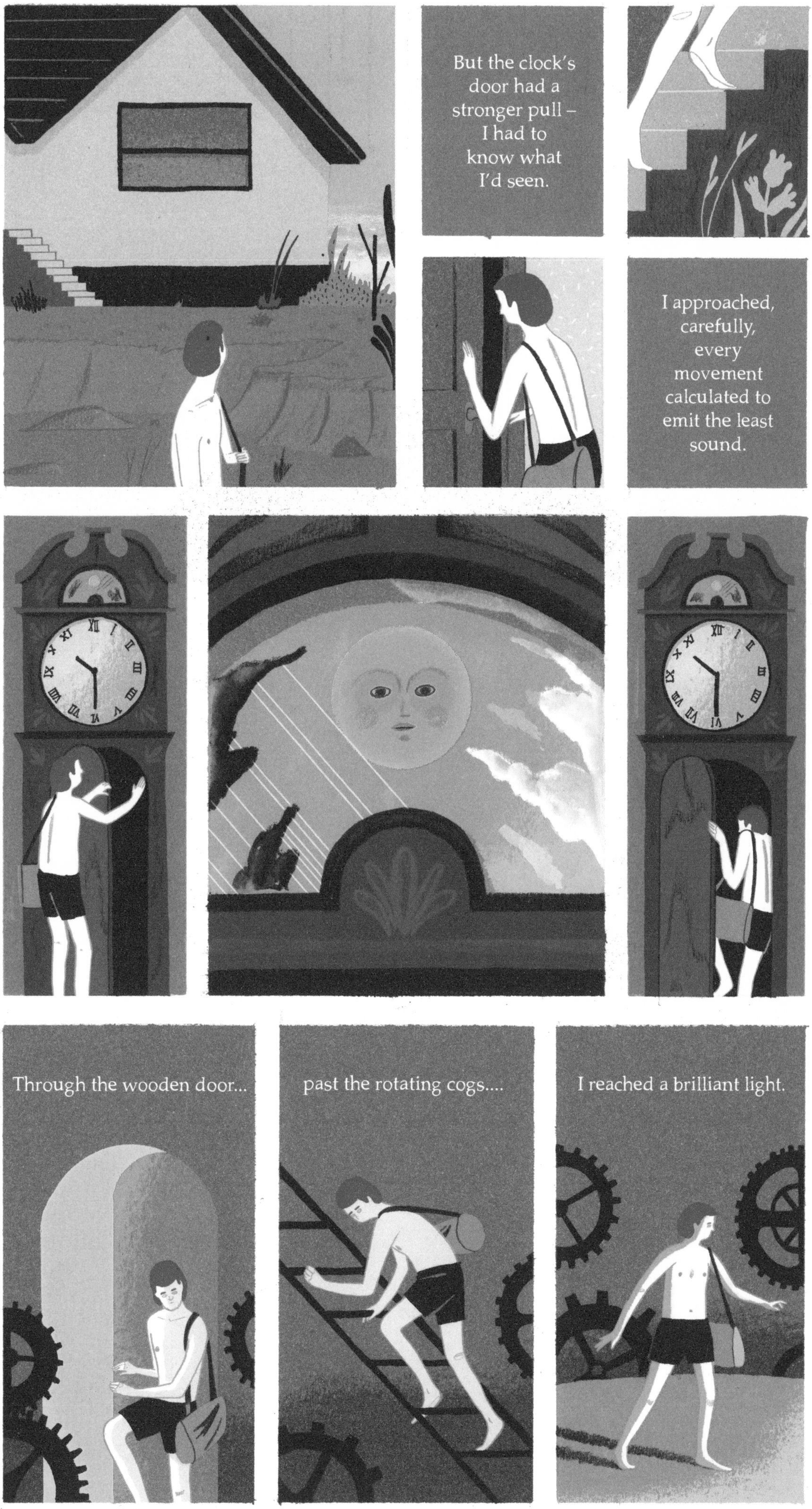
But the clock's door had a stronger pull – I had to know what I'd seen.
I approached, carefully, every movement calculated to emit the least sound.
Through the wooden door...
past the rotating cogs....
I reached a brilliant light.

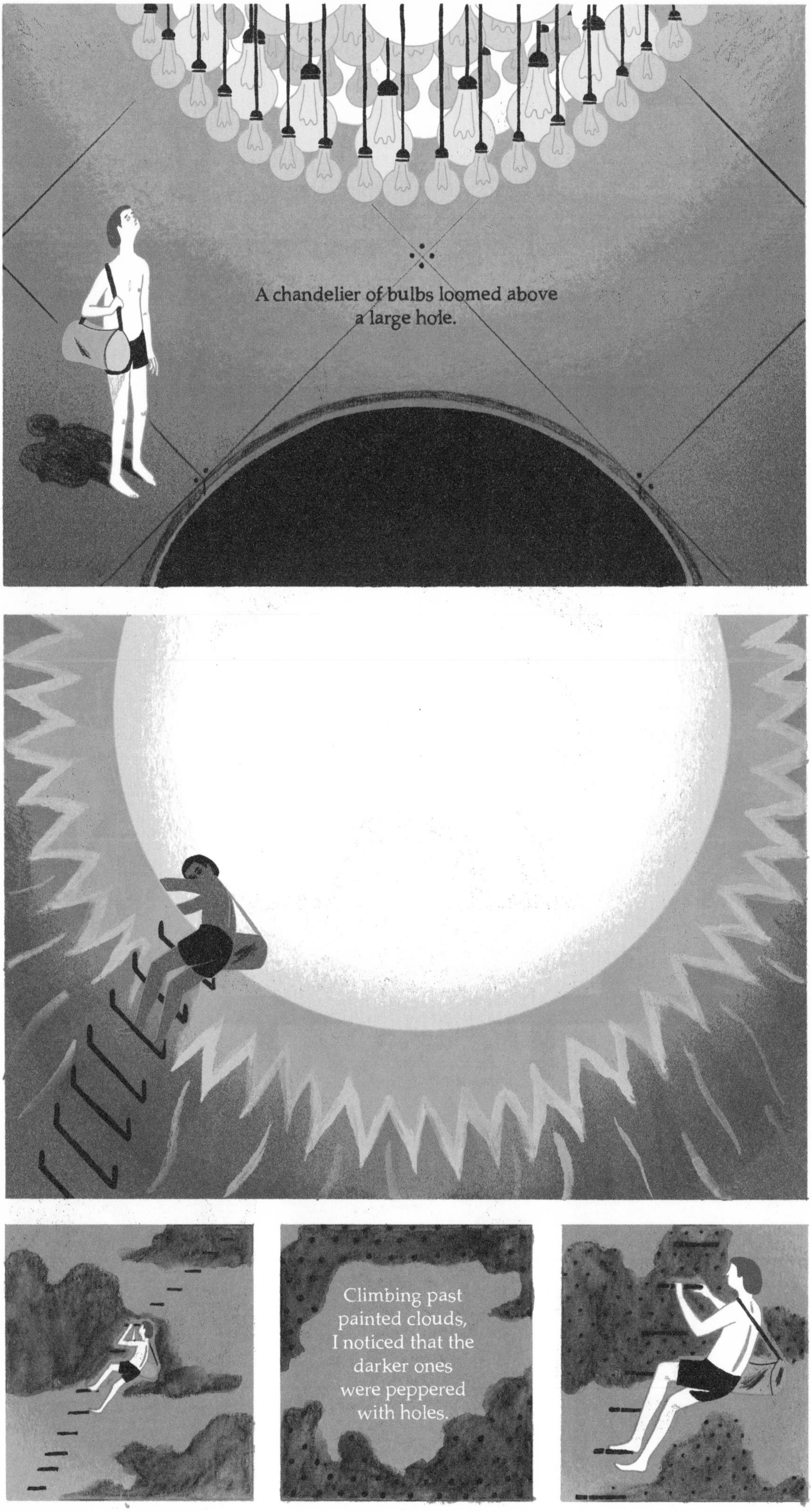
A chandelier of bulbs loomed above a large hole.
Climbing past painted clouds, I noticed that the darker ones were peppered with holes.

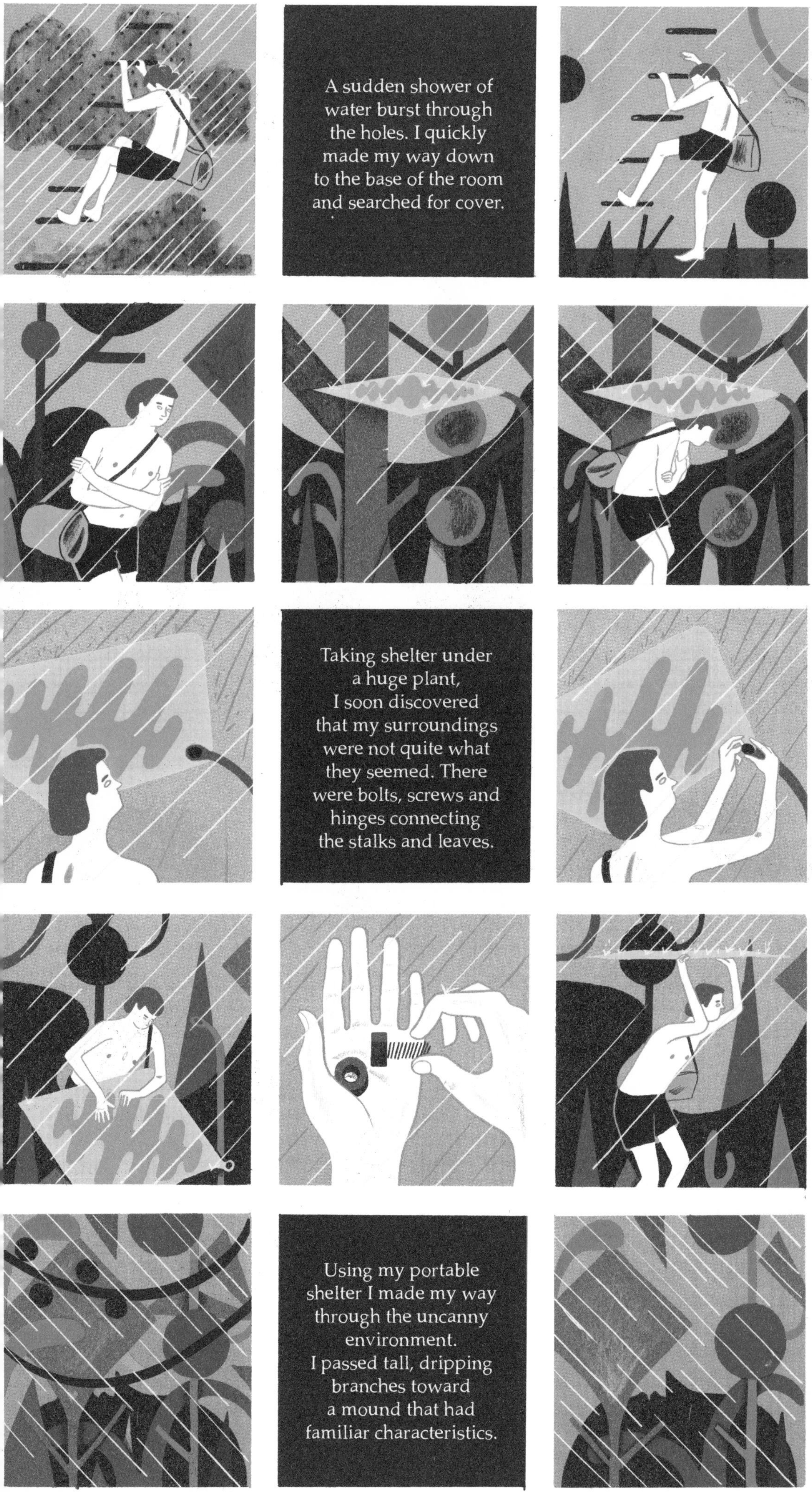
A sudden shower of water burst through the holes. I quickly made my way down to the base of the room and searched for cover.
Taking shelter under a huge plant, I soon discovered that my surroundings were not quite what they seemed. There were bolts, screws and hinges connecting the stalks and leaves.
Using my portable shelter I made my way through the uncanny environment. I passed tall, dripping branches toward a mound that had familiar characteristics.

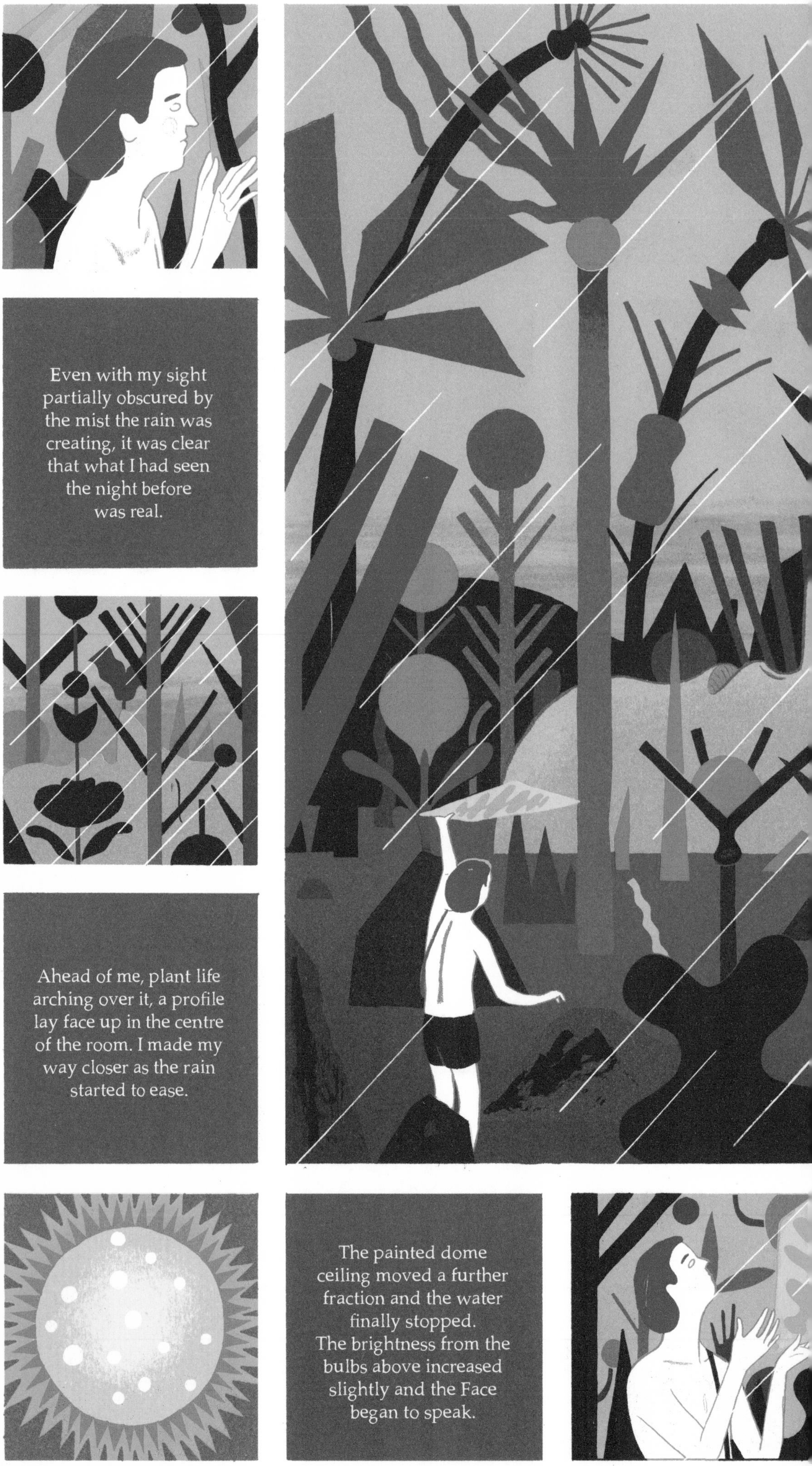
Even with my sight partially obscured by the mist the rain was creating, it was clear that what I had seen the night before was real.
Ahead of me, plant life arching over it, a profile lay face up in the centre of the room. I made my way closer as the rain started to ease.
The painted dome ceiling moved a further fraction and the water finally stopped. The brightness from the bulbs above increased slightly and the Face began to speak.

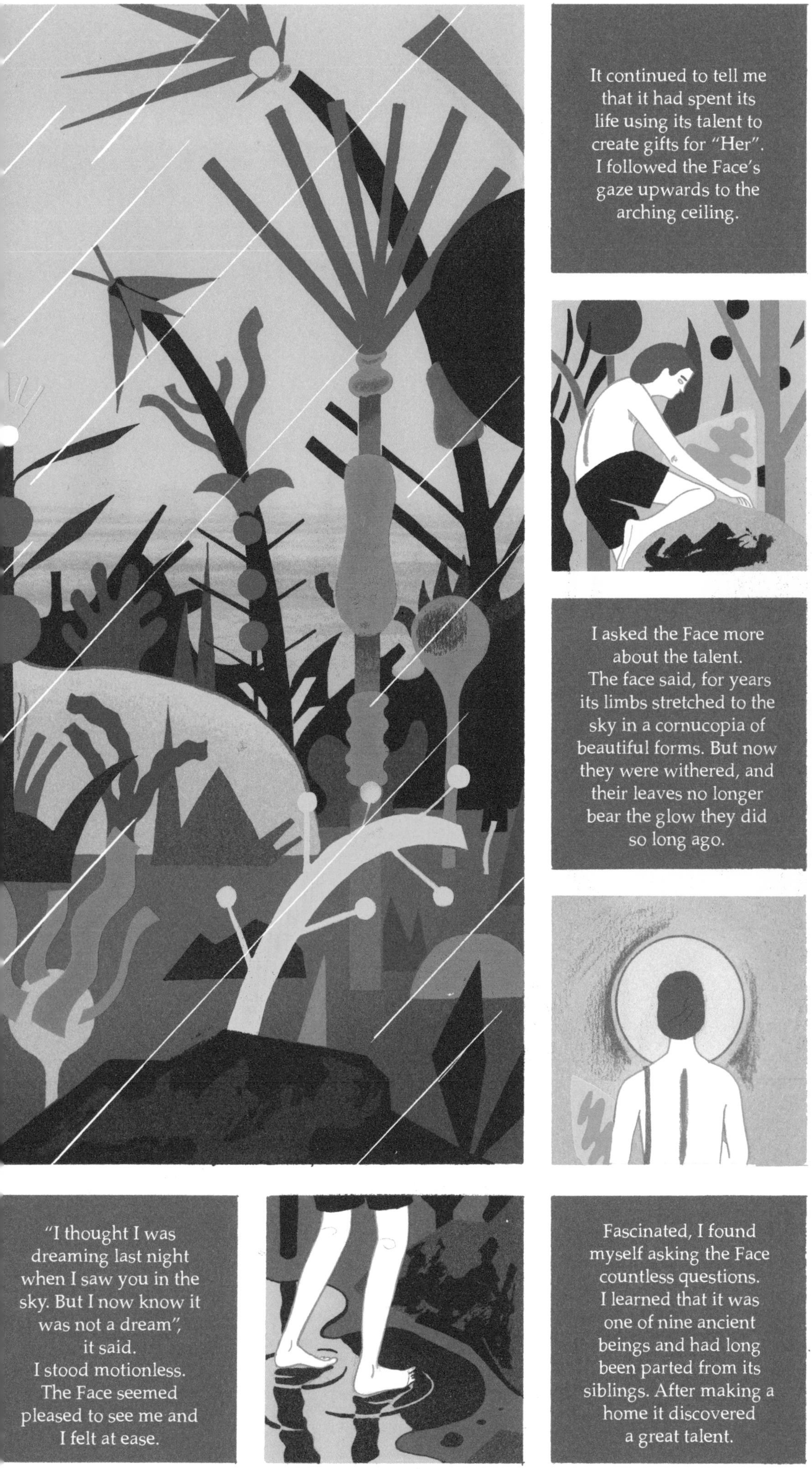
"I thought I was dreaming last night when I saw you in the sky. But I now know it was not a dream", it said. I stood motionless. The Face seemed pleased to see me and I felt at ease.
Fascinated, I found myself asking the Face countless questions. I learned that it was one of nine ancient beings and had long been parted from its siblings. After making a home it discovered a great talent.
It continued to tell me that it had spent its life using its talent to create gifts for "Her". I followed the Face's gaze upwards to the arching ceiling.
I asked the Face more about the talent. The face said, for years its limbs stretched to the sky in a cornucopia of beautiful forms. But now they were withered, and their leaves no longer bear the glow they did so long ago.

The Face was infatuated with the sun above. Always referring to it as "her", the Face told me how at first it was greeted so warmly by her. All his gifts blossomed as she accepted them, and as she drew closer, they multiplied in beauty and number. Then, with a pained expression, he said: "One day I awoke to see that she had drifted further away"

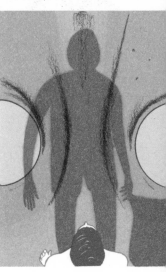

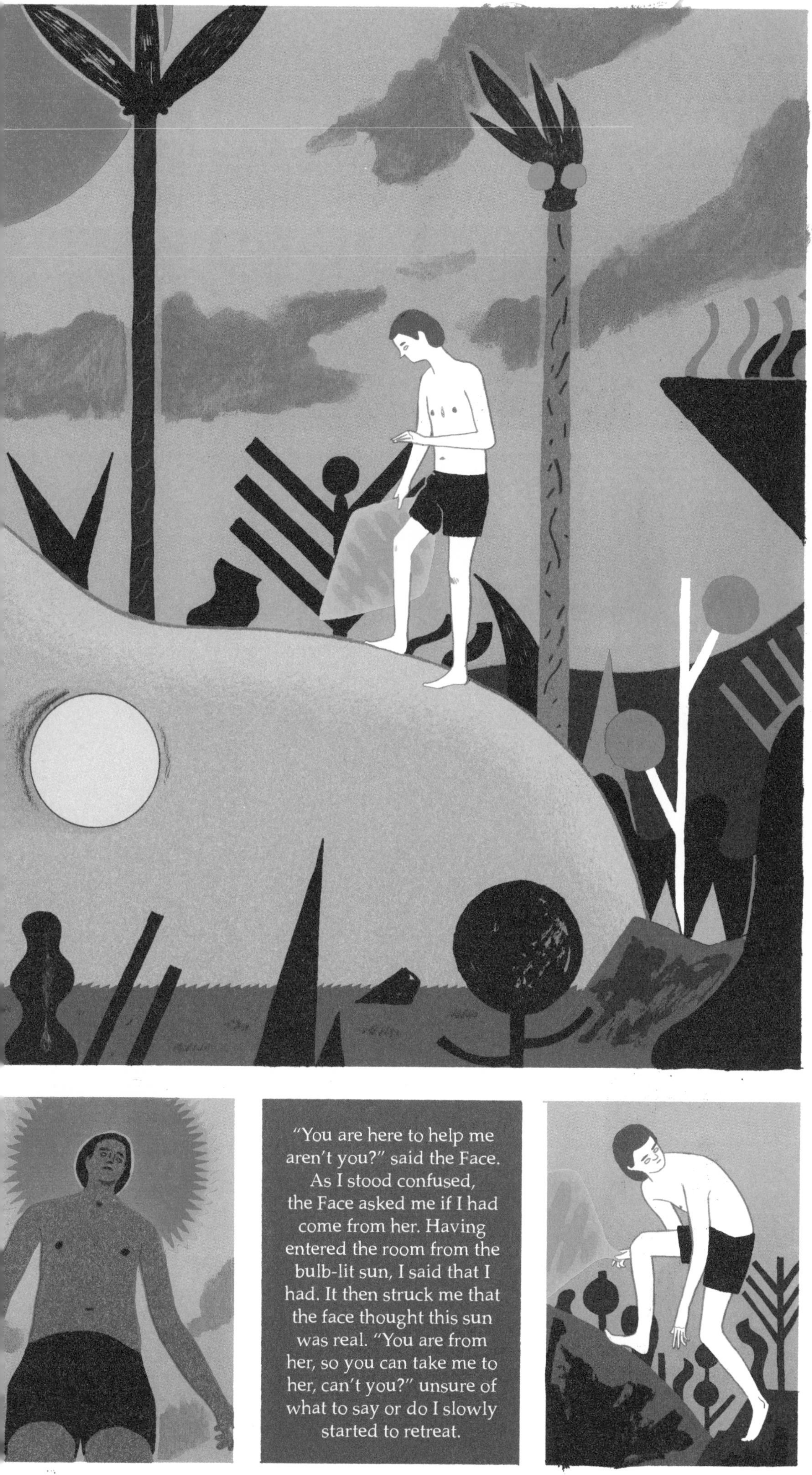
"You are here to help me aren't you?" said the Face. As I stood confused, the Face asked me if I had come from her. Having entered the room from the bulb-lit sun, I said that I had. It then struck me that the face thought this sun was real. "You are from her, so you can take me to her, can't you?" unsure of what to say or do I slowly started to retreat.

"I watch her pass over me every day, and she doesn't see me anymore, can't you help?" Said the Face.

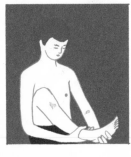

As I timidly explained that, as much as I liked, I didn't know how to help, I stumbled over something brittle.

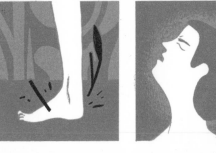

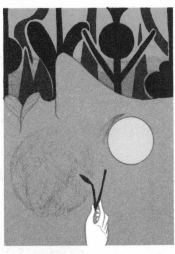

"You are already helping" announced the Face in excitement. It explained that it had not made anything grow since the sun had left, and now, with my arrival, something new had been created. It was the twig that I had dropped the previous night. I brought it closer to the Face.

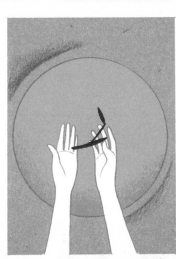

It was an amazing sight to see. The Face brought life to the small, lifeless twig. The awesome sight almost distracted me from the dimming light, Frank would be getting worried soon. Placing the new gift with the Face, I left with the excitment of having made a new friend.

Not wanting to disappoint my new friend, I departed with a half-truth (and a heavy conscience).

I told the Face that I was returning to the Sun to tell her about the new creation that he had just nurtured.

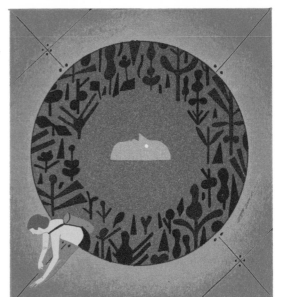

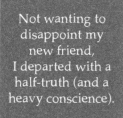

When I returned to my world above, the Face did not leave my thoughts, and I was keen to get back and see its progress with my twig as soon as I could.

At dinner I thought about questioning Frank.

I thought about what the Face had told me...

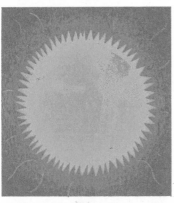

but I decided to find out more from the Face first.

Above the faux world beneath, I thought about the delight brought on by my unintentional gift. Small as it was, it did seem to help. I wanted to help more and had to get back soon.

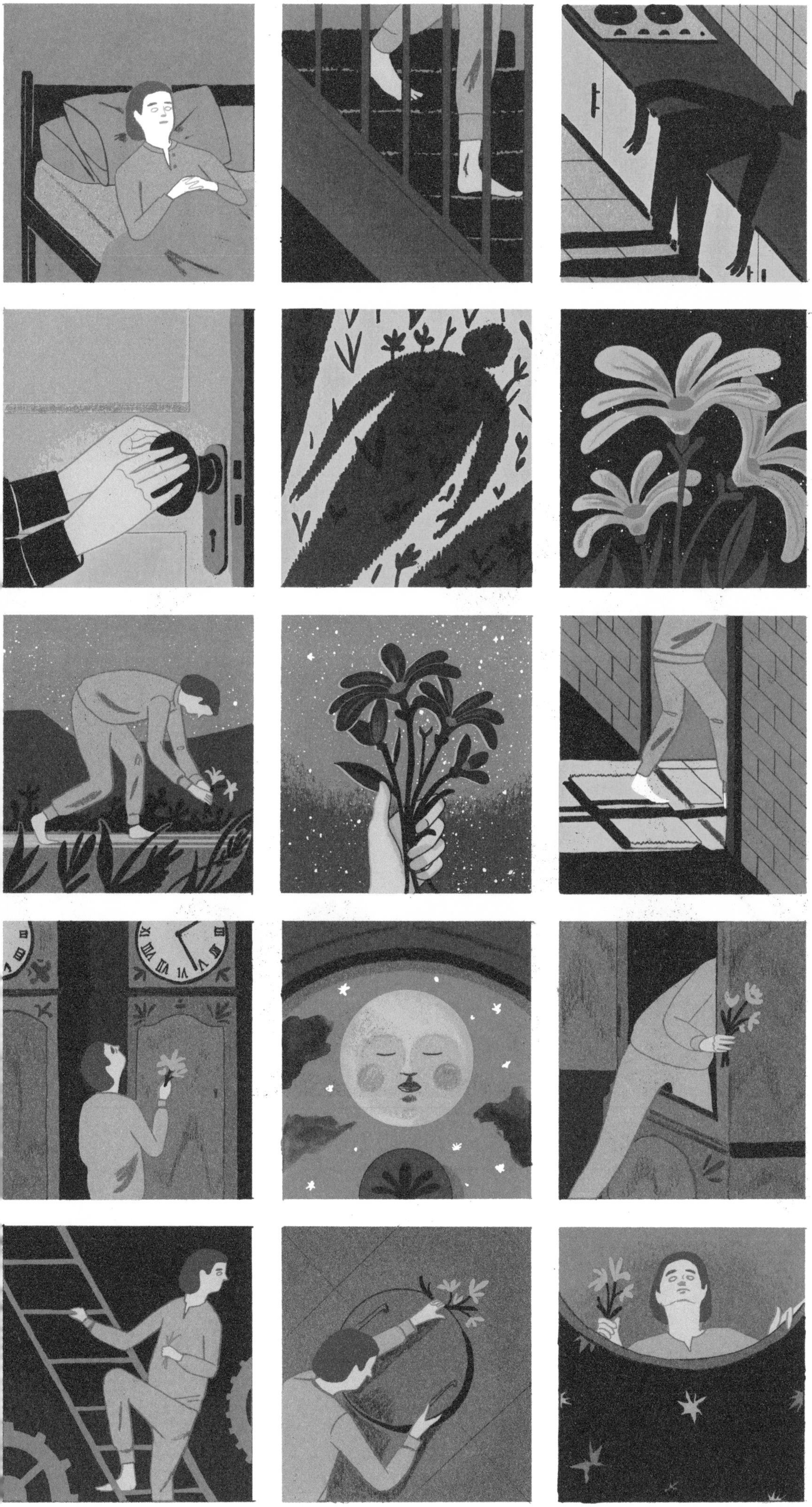

Upon my return with some fresher examples of the world above, I heard sobbing. The arched ceiling echoed with cries and muttering.

The face was distraught. It said that the sun was ignoring its new gift. It was dying. It didn't understand why its efforts had gone unnoticed.

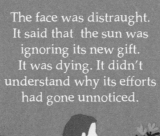

I realised that without the real sun the Face's efforts would always perish.

Before I had offered them, the flowers in my hand burst into life around me.

In a hysterical state, the Face took hold of me, rambling: "She accepted my gifts for so long, but never me, and just when she was in my reach she turned away."

There was nothing I could do but part from the Face immediately.

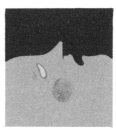

My struggle caused the Face more pain as it continued to beg and plead for my help.

Out of breath
and shaken,
I tried to think
of how I could
help my friend.

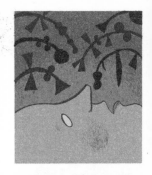

If only I could
prevent the
clocks from
being wound,
they would
slow and stop.

That would
bring the painted
sky to a halt,
and if I timed it
right it would be
daytime, always.

The Face would
get the Sun's
eternal attention.
First I needed
to take Frank's
winding key.

I couldn't help but regret disturbing the Face. My presence seemed to have only brought it distress.

I wanted to relieve its pain as quickly as I could so I set about retrieving the key that night.

I couldn't be certain when the clocks would stop so I turned off Frank's morning alarm.

This would grant me the time I needed. Time for my plan to take action.

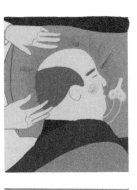

I hoped to talk to Frank about everything afterwards. My responsibility to stop the Face's suffering took priority.

I gently lifted the key from around his neck, quietly crept to my room and lay still, waiting for both suns to rise again.

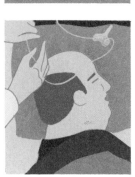

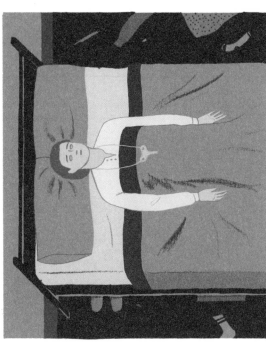

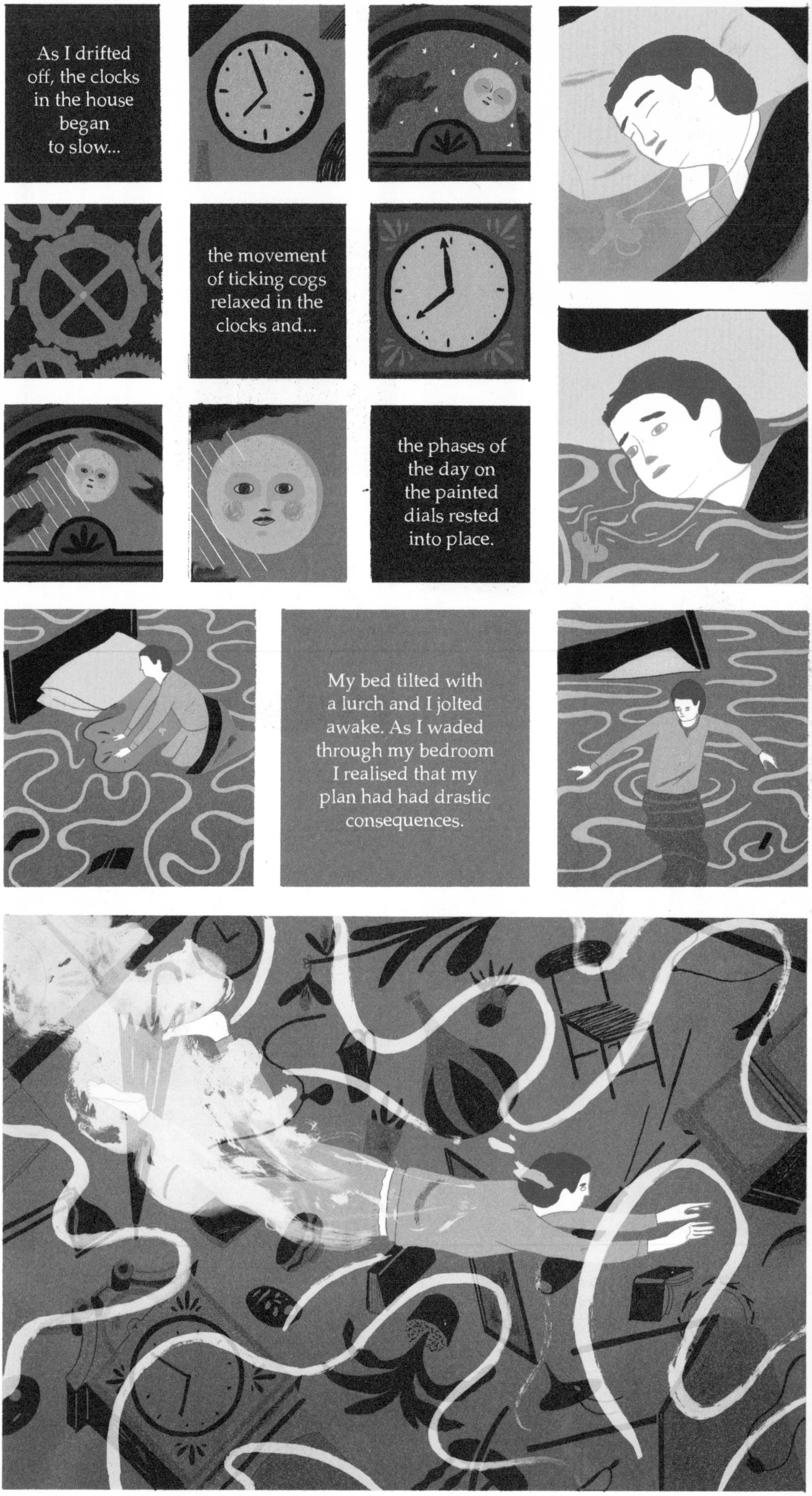

As I drifted off, the clocks in the house began to slow...
the movement of ticking cogs relaxed in the clocks and...
the phases of the day on the painted dials rested into place.
My bed tilted with a lurch and I jolted awake. As I waded through my bedroom I realised that my plan had had drastic consequences.

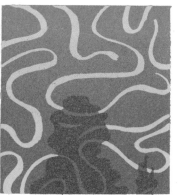

The point on which the clocks had stopped had set the painted sky-dome to rain.
The flood poured out of the house and into the surrounding valley.
My most recent pyjama swimming lesson became all too useful.

As I caught my breath I observed the landscape altered.

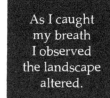

A trail of colour could be seen resting on the hills.

An approaching figure glided closer and picked me up.

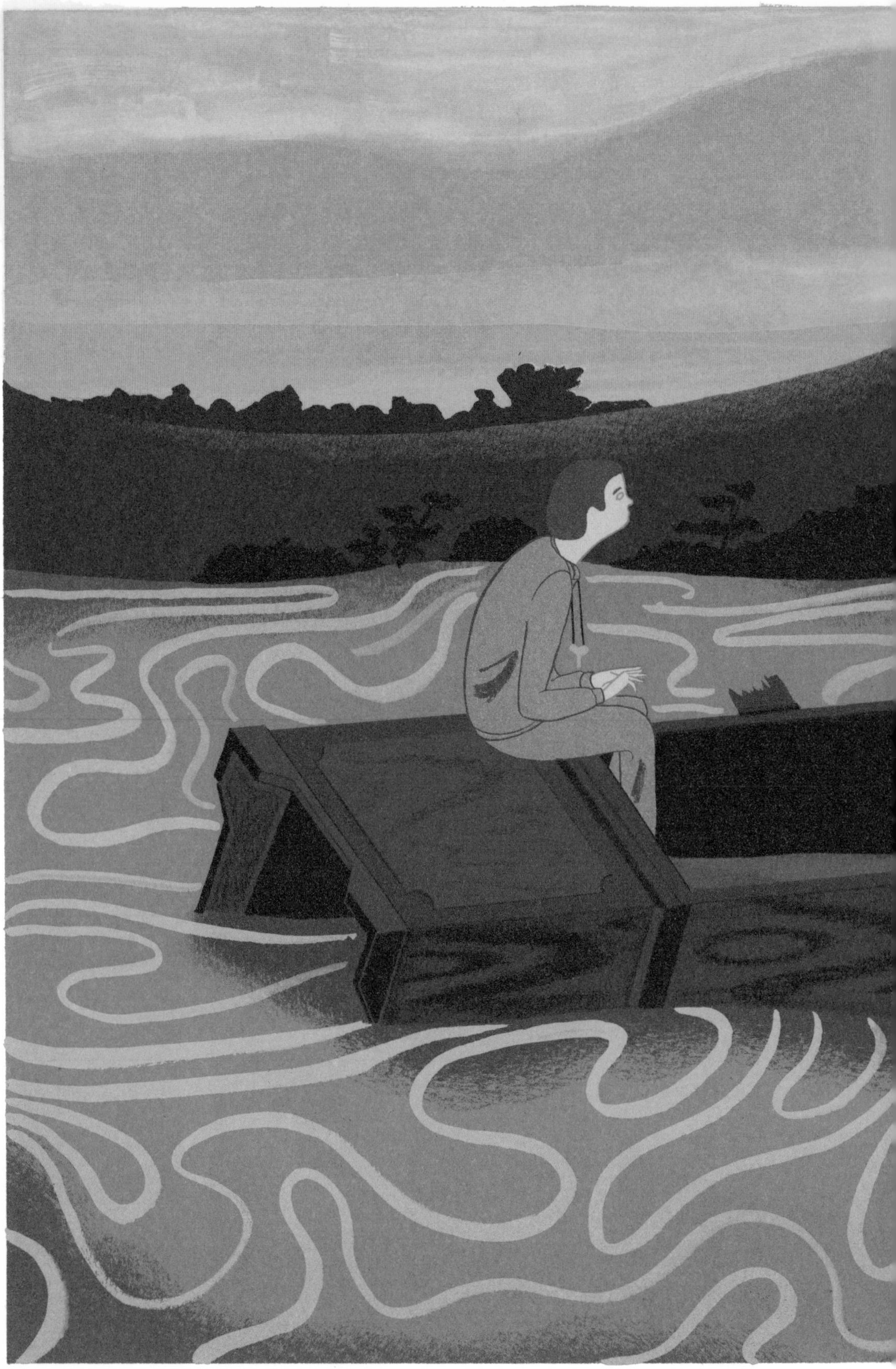

I was relieved to see that Frank was OK. He started to paddle towards the trail of colour on the distant hill. Concentrating on the journey, Frank occasionally looked back at me as he spoke about the Face. I was told that I would have found out about the clocks and the Face one day, as the responsibility was to be passed down to me. The Face had been found some time ago and was responsible for creating beautiful forms from beneath the early terrain of the earth. Our great ancestors found it in an entwining Eden where its lush surroundings reached tall into the sky. Transfixed on the sun above, everything else became invisible to it.

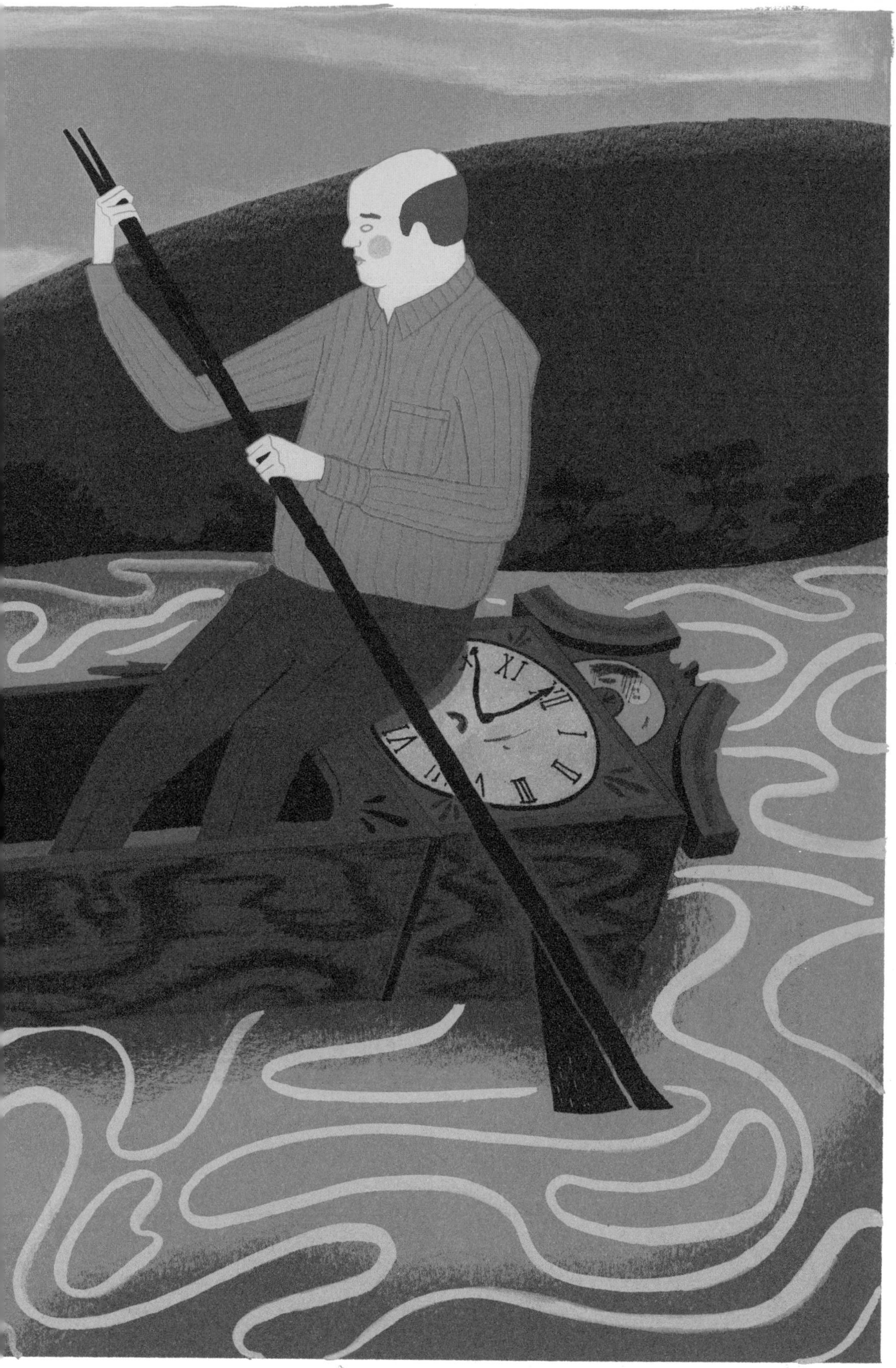

Such was the power of the Face and its obsession with the Sun that it pulled the Earth closer to the Sun day by day. Unable to interrupt this, a decision was made to forge a less obedient environment and sever the Face's gaze.

The dome had been built by our ancestors in the hope that the Face would eventually forget about its obsession and be released. But, unable to forego its feelings and merely take joy in its outstanding creations, the Face was entombed in a crepuscule and the responsibility to maintain the life-saving farce fell upon their descendants. Ever since, the clocks would have to be wound the same way every morning to keep the semblance of day and night alive and to keep the Face from pulling all of its hard work, and us, into the blazing Sun.

As we approached the shore, Frank was eager to see the Face.

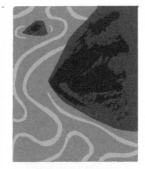

A trail of large flowers led us up a tall hill, and I could sense a wild presence ahead.

We parted through the last layer of the Face's new limbs to reveal it basking in the light.

Before Frank and I had time to discuss what to do, I had alerted the Face's attention.

"I have her attention again, and she is on her way." said the face and it thanked me.

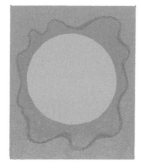

It told me that my arrival had brought back its talent to create.

Frank asked me how it was that I had the Face's attention and could speak to it.

I whispered that it thought I was from the Sun. Frantically, Frank put his hand on my shoulder...

Frank grabbed me and exclaimed that if the Face listened to me then I could trap it again.

The Face misinterpreted Frank's movements as a threat to me and it took hold of him.

 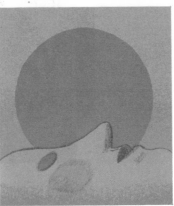 

In panic I pleaded with the Face to let Frank go, but its thoughts were elsewhere. "She is leaving me again" it said over and over. The Sun was setting.

I noticed that the Sun was setting over the ocean.

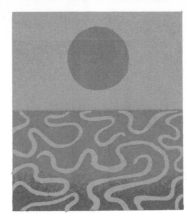

I told the Face that the Sun lived in the sea.

The Face trusted me and it began to rise from the mound.

The ground tremored and the Face started making its way to the water. I sprinted ahead, as if to lead the way.

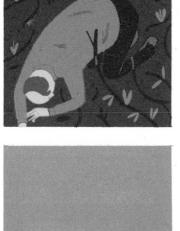

As the Face met the water a change was visible.

The Face controlled the water like it did the earth.

The Face continued to try and pull the Sun closer, this resulted in the Face shifting the ocean and itself towards the horizon.

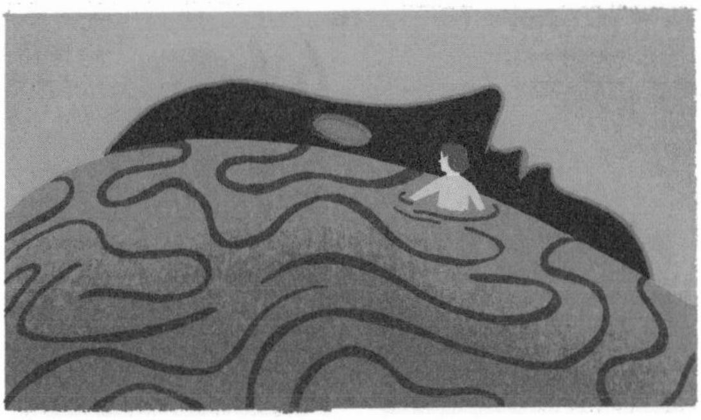

I said to the Face that the Sun rests in the sea every night and that she would be waiting there for him if he travelled the distance.

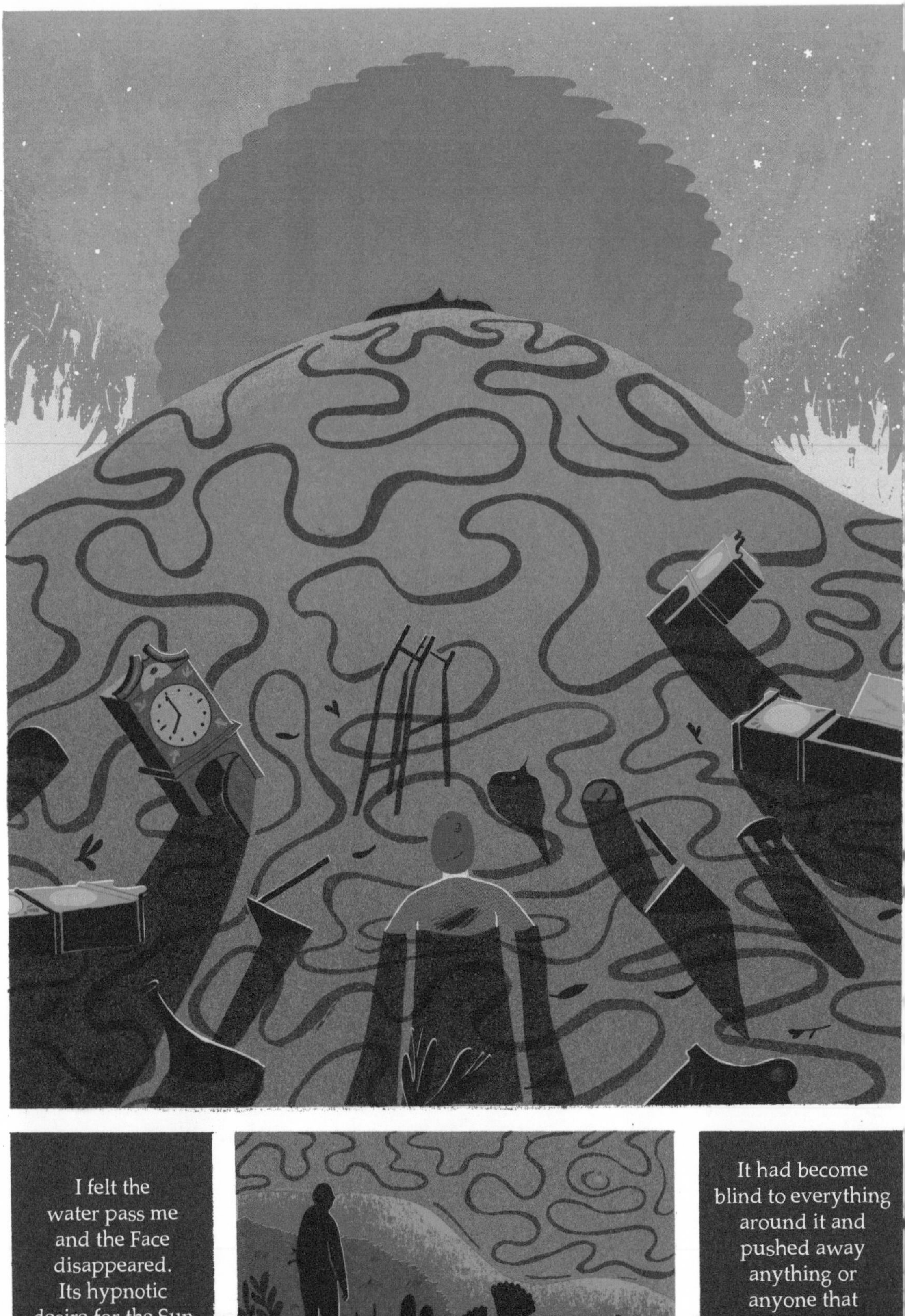

I felt the water pass me and the Face disappeared. Its hypnotic desire for the Sun had no end.

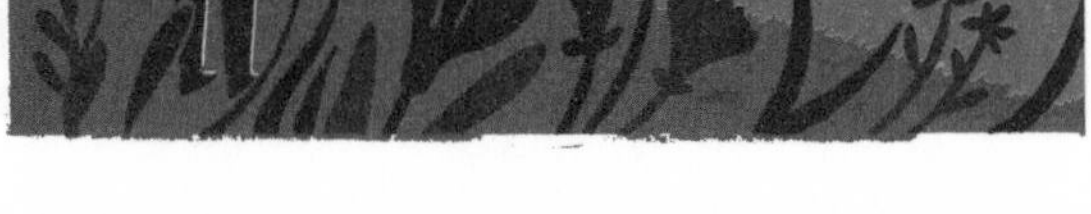

It had become blind to everything around it and pushed away anything or anyone that couldn't help it reach her.

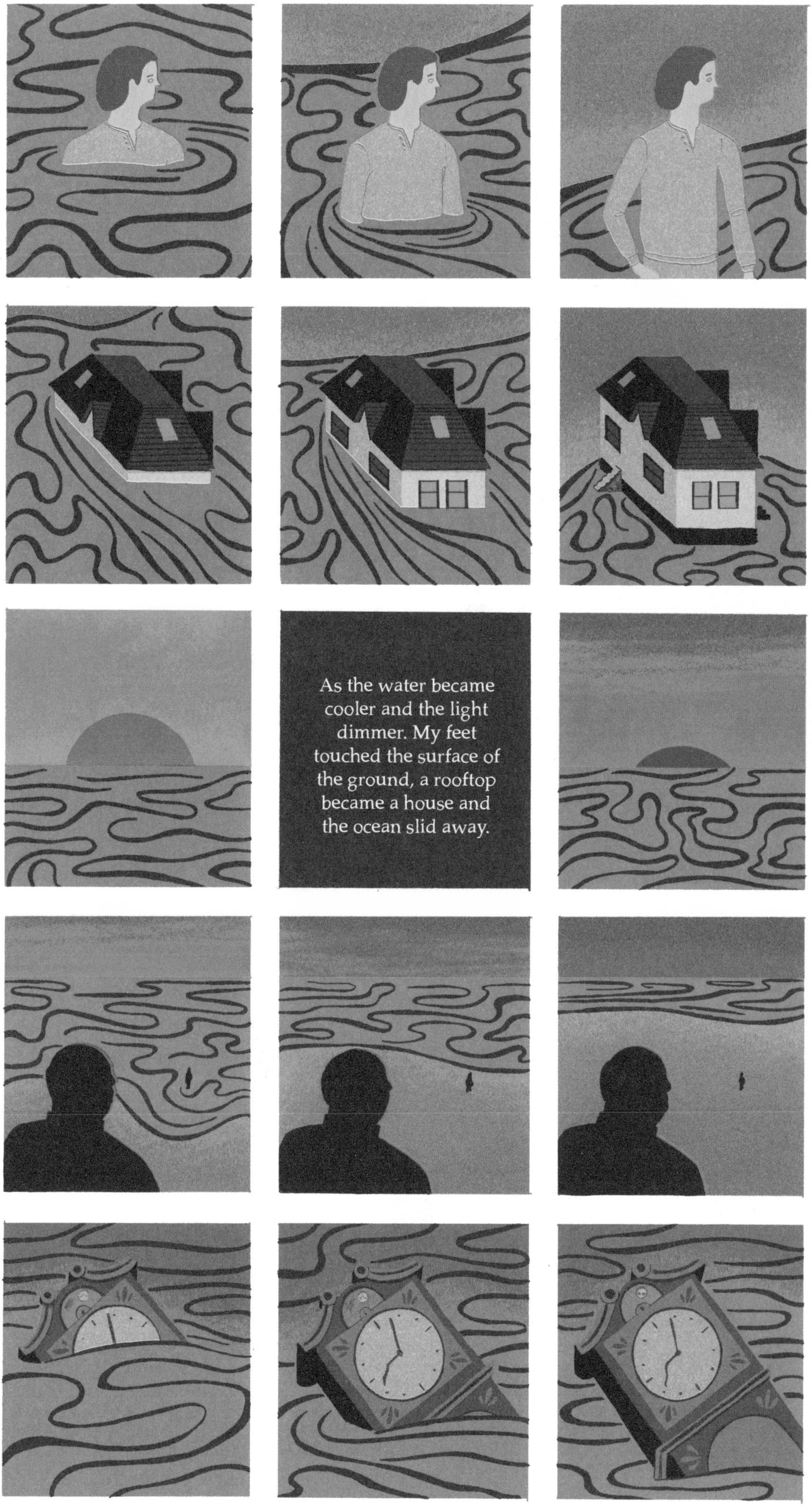
As the water became cooler and the light dimmer. My feet touched the surface of the ground, a rooftop became a house and the ocean slid away.

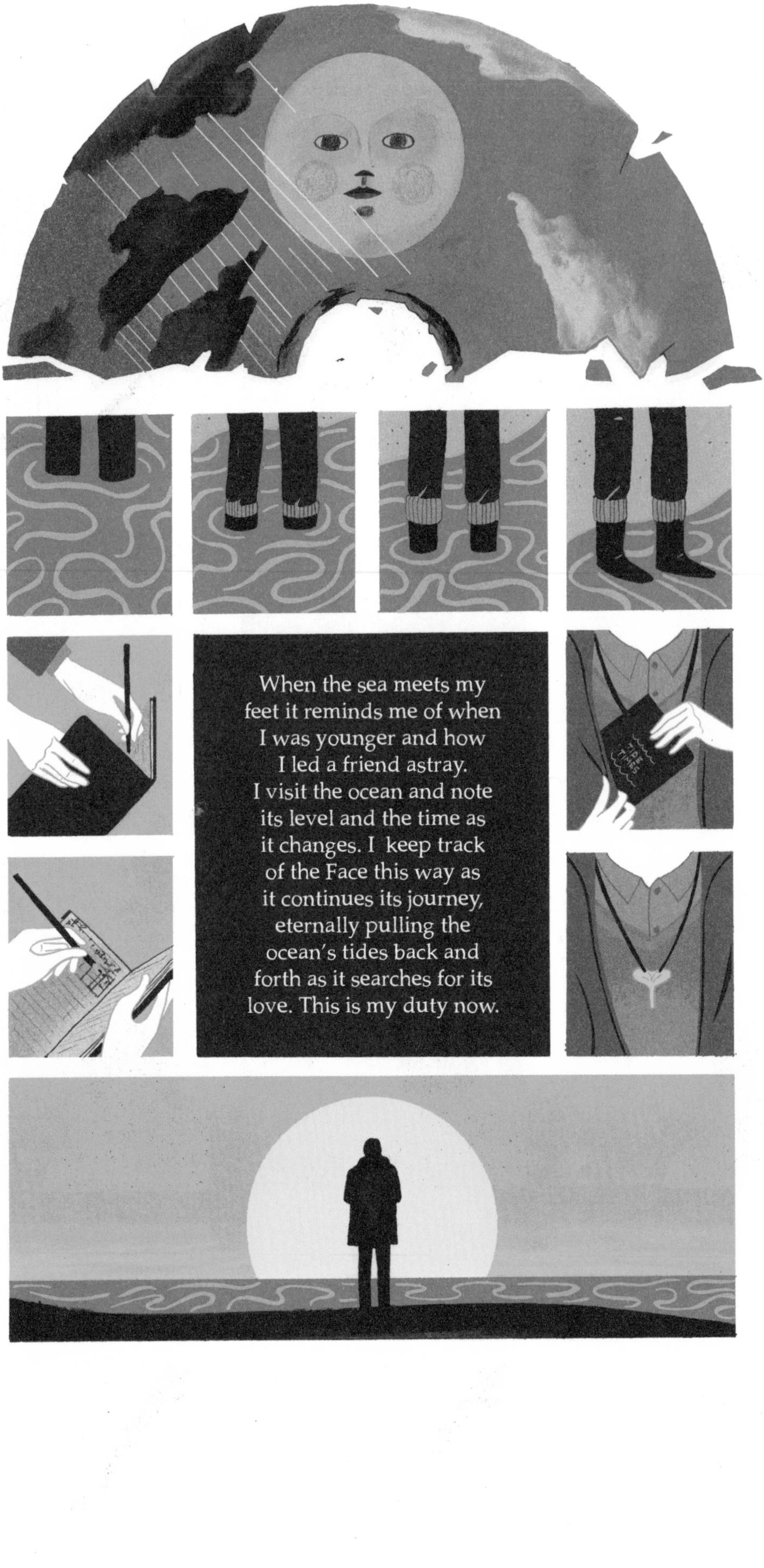
When the sea meets my feet it reminds me of when I was younger and how I led a friend astray. I visit the ocean and note its level and the time as it changes. I keep track of the Face this way as it continues its journey, eternally pulling the ocean's tides back and forth as it searches for its love. This is my duty now.
TIDE TIMES

This is a first edition printed in 2013.

Published by Nobrow Ltd. 62 Great Eastern Street, London, EC2A 3QR
Printed in Belgium on FSC assured paper
ISBN: 978-1-907704-61-1
Order from nobrow.net

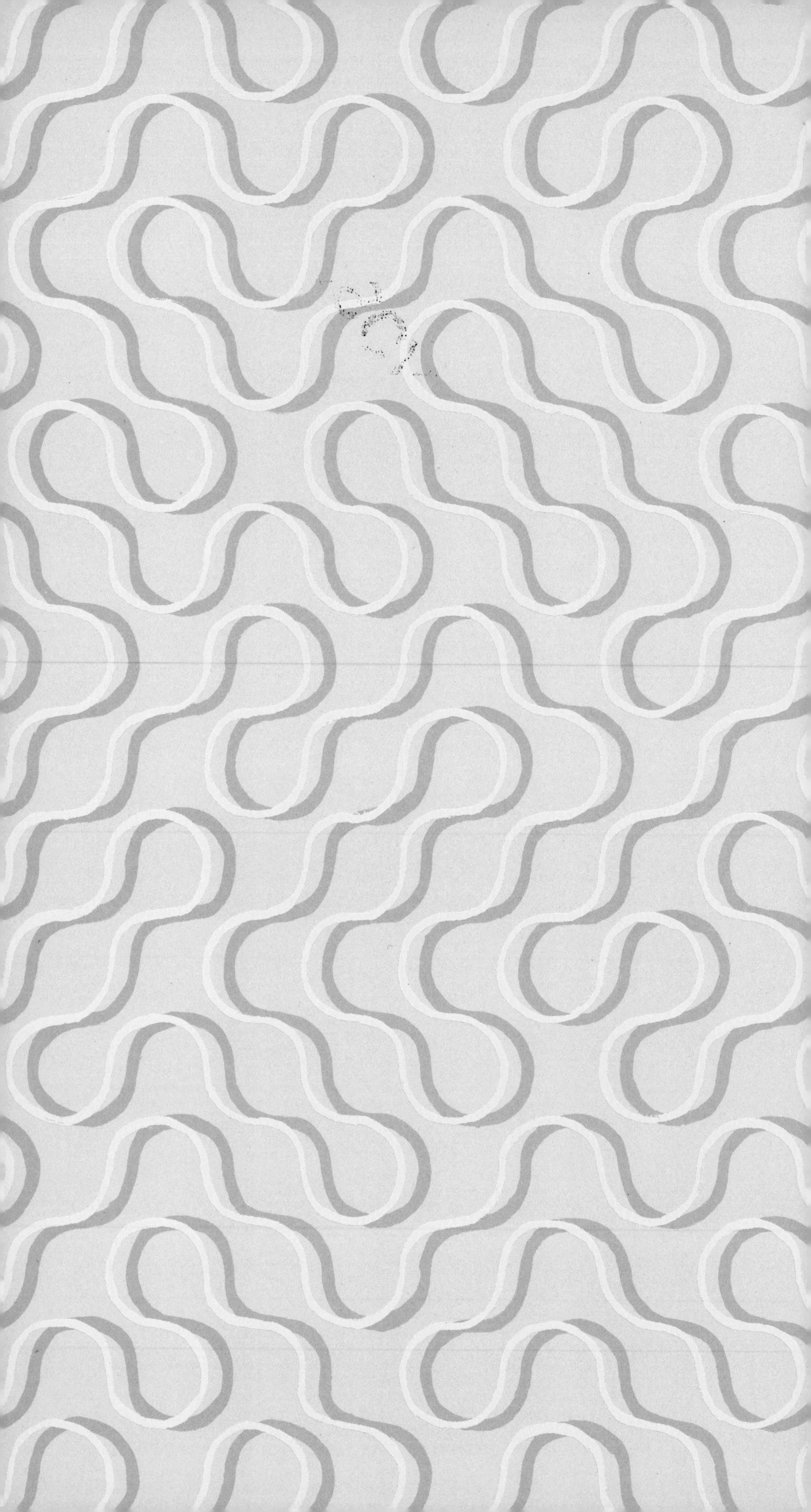